Hellenic Studies 66

PLATO'S WAYWARD PATH

Recent Titles in the Hellenic Studies Series

http://chs.harvard.edu/chs/publications

PLATO'S WAYWARD PATH

LITERARY FORM AND THE *REPUBLIC*

David Schur

CENTER FOR HELLENIC STUDIES
Trustees for Harvard University
Washington, D.C.
Distributed by Harvard University Press
Cambridge, Massachusetts, and London, England
2014

Dedicated to the memory of Dorrit Cohn

Contents

Preface

"You have degraded what should have been a course of lectures into a series of tales."

> Sir Arthur Conan Doyle,
> "The Adventure of the Copper Beeches"

THIS LITTLE BOOK reconsiders literary form in Plato from a methodological perspective. It inquires into Plato's methods of writing and it addresses modern methods of reading Plato. In order to treat the problem of literary form in a coherent and responsible manner, I have found it beneficial to limit the scope of the book rather severely.[1] From a historical perspective, the main limitation of my approach is that it does not seek to recover *Platonism* from Plato's writings. From a methodological point of view, however, this is an advantageous starting point, as it allows a wider range of verbal patterns to be discerned in specific texts. I do not see Plato assuming the position of a knower in his writings. Nor do I see any particular consistency throughout the dialogues in Plato's attitude toward specific topics; exhibiting the preoccupations of an extraordinarily fertile mind, Plato considers many different problems from many different angles.[2]

The work presented here grew out of a long-standing interest in the relationship between literary metaphor and hermeneutic method (see Schur 1998). Around the turn of the millennium, I was fortunate enough to have a good many discussions about the *Republic* with the narrative theorist Dorrit Cohn, who was learning ancient Greek and had become intrigued by Socrates' peculiar

---

[1] On risk and responsibility in the peculiarly challenging enterprise of interpreting Plato's books, see Tigerstedt 1977:107–108.

[2] The sort of passion that interpreters observe in Socrates and Plato (e.g. Rowe 2006:9) is no more indicative of consistent argumentation and no more intense than is, say, James Joyce's lifelong interest in Dublin, Catholicism, and aesthetics. The problem may be observed in Kahn 1996; although he does not wish to treat "Plato's literary creations as if these were historical documents" (3), he does nonetheless want to treat them as philosophical documents, and "we cannot ascribe to Plato eighteen different philosophies" (37).

authority as the dominant speaker in most of Plato's dialogues. (Her work on Plato resulted in two articles, Cohn 2000 and 2001.) I then spent a year at the Center for Hellenic Studies in Washington, DC, where I tried to puzzle through the baffling phenomenon of indirect communication (a term favored by Kierkegaard) in Plato. Exploring the scholarship on Plato's use of literary form, I had the impression that something from the literary dimension was getting left out of the conversation, something that was difficult to articulate. At the same time, I became increasingly convinced that the *Republic* is a (very unusual) work of narrative fiction, even though narratologists like Cohn and Genette had been reluctant to countenance this quirk of literary form because of the book's place in the canon of theoretical philosophy. It took roughly another ten years before I reached the understanding of these problems presented here.

The topic of literary form in Plato has attracted great interest from scholars during my lifetime, and this study seeks to further their efforts. The first half of the book is devoted to reconsidering the modern problem of literary form in Plato and to developing a coherent and, for the most part, broadly applicable response. The second half focuses on Plato's *Republic*, offering analyses of structure and wording. My reading of the dialogue is meant to demonstrate the potential benefits of an approach that gives priority to Plato's text by viewing the book as a depiction of a conversation. In general, this means separating the conversation and its goals from the book and its rhetorical portrayal of the conversation. I argue that the answers deemed most important in that conversation (most obviously, the Idea of the Good) are portrayed in the book as desired but absent, displaced by ongoing questioning. While my discussion of the *Republic* is by no means a comprehensive interpretation, it does offer a perspective on the dialogue as a whole. And although the two parts of the book shed light on each other, they are not strictly interdependent; one could read them as separate essays.

The main thrust of my argument in the first two chapters is that Plato's verbal compositions, when treated as literary, necessarily have significant and interesting functions apart from argumentative persuasion. Many scholars today share the conviction that literary features of Plato's writing style, features that used to be disregarded as mere decoration, are of integral significance. This is a modern view, fueled in the last century by the belief that style is inherently significant and also by the Freudian insight that wording is never innocent. The pursuit of a pure content, cloaked in transparent or decorative trappings, now seems naïve. In an attempt to justify Plato's style in the historically determined context of modern philosophy, however, many interpreters have turned to classical rhetoric as an answer, arguing that Plato's literary vagaries are rhetorical tactics, covertly serving his resolutely single-minded agenda. I question this answer, raising the objection that an instrumental conception of rhetoric, in which literary style remains subservient to content, ultimately perpetuates a view of style that ignores the waywardness of literariness itself.

In chapter 3, I suggest a possible way to move forward, using modern concepts of linguistics and literary rhetoric to develop an alternative model for understanding the function of literary features in Plato. Here I draw a positive conception of literariness from the previous two chapters' negative findings: literariness can be understood to encompass precisely those functions that complicate the communication of a univocal message. Whereas traditional rhetoric, by definition, studies the promotion of univocal authorial messages, modern (twentieth-century) literary-rhetorical analysis allows for multiple formal-thematic patterns in a single text. Accordingly, the literary features of Plato's dialogues—when treated *as* literary—cannot be limited to a single argumentative agenda. To demonstrate this point, I consider how the *Republic*, in a conspicuous rhetorical pattern of self-reflection, portrays a heuristic conversation while simultaneously emphasizing difficulties that prevent the conversation from reaching its goals. In short, the *Republic* qualifies the authority of its conclusions by displaying a strong countercurrent of ongoing movement.

Chapter 4 observes this current of ongoing movement in the distance traveled, by methodical paths, from the beginning to the end of the *Republic*. Socrates' narrative, the conversation he recounts, the investigation pursued by the conversation, and the methods that are a recurrent topic of investigation in the conversation—all are conceptualized as paths. And while the conversation strives toward fixed goals, its progress is qualified by the distance and the digressions traced by these paths. In chapters 5 and 6, two sequences of argumentation are examined: the conversation's inquiry into justice through the planning of an ideal regime, and Socrates' explanation of the Good by way of the Sun, Line, and Cave. Both sequences are shown to rely on *likenesses* that increase the distance between the seekers and their goals.

In sum, my overall argument concerning the *Republic* goes roughly as follows: Along with great abstract topics such as truth, justice, and political organization, the *Republic* is *about* a conversation. And in a continual, recursive movement of self-reflection to which Plato has bent the dialogue form, a major topic of that conversation is itself—the participants (Socrates and his companions) frequently reflect on their procedures and reconsider what they have said.[3] When viewed through the lens of traditional philosophy, which focuses on argumentation as the significant content of the communicative text, such

---

[3] "As so often in the *Republic*," comments Eva Brann on a particular point in the dialogue, "the conversation makes its own mode the object of reflection ..." (2004:160).

recursions are usually considered peripheral asides. But through this running metaconversational commentary, the conversation becomes a topic of conversation, and questions of method become matters of content. In this way, the *Republic* engages in self-criticism and methodological exploration, raising questions about the nature of conversational investigation, while the goals of that investigation remain surprisingly remote.

I thank the fellows and staff who made the Center for Hellenic Studies a terrific place to be in 2001–2002, the CHS publications team for their help in bringing this study to light, and colleagues who were kind enough to give some of these ideas a thoughtful hearing at annual meetings of the APA and CAMWS. I am especially grateful to my colleagues at Brooklyn College, The City University of New York, where a Whiting Fellowship gave me extra time to work on this book. Various forms of assistance at different stages came from Hans Beck, Casey Dué, Mary Ebbott, David Greetham, Sean Kelsey, Lenny Muellner, Gregory Nagy, Nickolas Pappas, James Pletcher, Gerald Press, Jill Curry Robbins, Jennifer Roberts, Peter Rose, John Van Sickle, David Weeks, and Liv Yarrow. I am ever thankful to the following for their general support: Kevin McLaughlin, Sandra Naddaff, Marc Shell, Marina Van Zuylen, and Lori Yamato. I dedicate this book to the memory of Dorrit Cohn.

Part 1

Literary Form and Classical Rhetoric

1

The Problem of Literary Form

WE RARELY ASK WHY Sophocles composed tragedies; Dickens, novels; or Dickinson, poems. These writers were presumably driven to these genres by psychological and cultural forces about which it would seem idle to speculate. When it comes to Plato, however, why he chose to write as he did has long been a serious question, becoming even more insistent in the modern era. "Why did Plato choose precisely this form?" asked W. G. Tennemann in his *System of Platonic Philosophy*, published in 1792.[1] The question has persisted into the twenty-first century.[2] In this chapter, my concern is with some of the most prominent ways that the question has been answered, while the next chapter deals with some general but crucial methodological assumptions that commonly guide the modern interpretation of literary form in Plato's dialogues. I find that the prevalent view of literary form as philosophical rhetoric is marred by a methodological confusion between expository and literary conceptions of discourse.

Baldly stated, this chapter argues that the notion of persuasive rhetoric applies readily to expository discourse but not to Plato's dialogues. The dialogues are widely recognized to be manifestly, and sometimes pronouncedly, *not* expository in form. Efforts to interpret the dialogues in terms of persuasive rhetoric are therefore compromised by insuperable methodological challenges. In the chapters following this one, I will continue to address the problem of literary form, while turning toward Plato's *Republic* and engaging with textual evidence from that dialogue. My analysis will describe recursion as a master trope in the *Republic*, but one whose function is to diffuse or modalize rather than promote univocal positions, modalization being a function that has little in common with traditional rhetoric.

---

[1] Tennemann 1792:127 (*Warum wählte Plato gerade diese Form ... ?*); translation by the author. Tigerstedt 1977:67 calls Tennemann's book "the first modern monograph on Plato." See also Szlezák 1997, Lamm 2000.

[2] English-language variations of the question may be found in, e.g., Scott 2007:xviii, Rowe 2007:25, Blondell 2002:38, Cooper 1997:xviii; Rutherford 1995:8; Sayre 1995; Griswold 2002:1, 143.

Schleiermacher's Model of Unified Form and Content

Although Tennemann saw much that was good about the dialogue form chosen by Plato, which he called a delightful kind of "philosophical drama," he nevertheless considered this aspect of Plato's writing an aesthetic indulgence, ultimately inessential and potentially distracting (126–127). The "course of investigation" (*der Gang der Untersuchung*), presented in the dialogue form favored by Plato, can lead readers astray. It often encourages readers "to wander from the topic" (*von dem Gegenstande abzuschweifen*, 127). The topic (*Gegenstand*) under investigation, the "system of Platonic philosophy" announced by Tennemann's title, thus becomes markedly distinct from the subject matter that the reader encounters directly, which may involve characters doing things in various locations and defending different positions in rational argument. Indeed, the dialogue form can make it difficult for readers "to distinguish the authentic topic (*den eigentlichen Gegenstand*) from the incidental, to grasp the correct viewpoint, and to find the authentic results" (127). So the reader who follows Plato's written dialogues is at risk of getting lost, adopting incorrect viewpoints along the way, and reaching inauthentic results. Tennemann presumes to speak as one who has already found the authentic results that readers seek, and now that more than two hundred years have passed, some may be tempted to focus on the evident dogmatism of Tennemann's concern. Yet the imagined object of study that is Plato's authentic philosophy is by no means directly accessible through his writings. Tennemann's expert warning reflects a disturbing and persistent problem: perhaps Plato's style of writing obscures, rather than reveals, his real, authentic, actual message. To observe a separation between style (i.e. form) and message (content), as Tennemann does, is also to set appearance against reality. Form can mask, or even masquerade as, content, while content itself remains hidden from view. Conceptually, the preinstalled, retrievable message—the result of studying the object (which must be viewed correctly for the real topic to be seen)—is mediated by the thinker's writing, and this mediation can be a kind of distraction from the author's position.

Tennemann's main successor in the world of Platonic scholarship, Friedrich Schleiermacher, explained the role of dialogue form quite differently, by emphasizing its purposefulness (*Absichtlichkeit*) and connectedness (*Zusammenhang*), and this view has made a vital contribution to the modern study of Plato.[3] Each dialogue, Schleiermacher argued, is an organic composition in which each part and every detail, when understood in its context, serves Plato's global philosophical purpose. In his "General Introduction" to Plato's dialogues, first

---

[3]   See Klein 1965:3–10, Krämer 1990:3–74, Szlezák 1997, Lamm 2000.

published in 1804, Schleiermacher laments various misunderstandings of Plato.[4] Schleiermacher is especially keen-sighted in identifying Plato's writings themselves as a major cause of widespread and enduring misunderstanding of Plato's thought. Even those who recognize Plato's greatness, he says, have trouble reconciling their esteem for the thinker with their impression of his writings—"the two will not agree"—because the writings appear to suffer from contradiction (*Widerspruch*) and disconnectedness (*Unzusammenhang*); such readers see the dialogue form as "a quite-useless and more-confusing-than-illuminating embellishment of the perfectly common way of presenting thoughts" (1836:8–9). We may safely assume that the common type of philosophical presentation meant here is the expository treatise or speech: a declarative, consistent, and linear presentation of an author's propositions. Schleiermacher says that complaints about Plato's unusual form of presentation may be resolved by demonstrating a holistic connectedness (*Zusammenhang*) in the dialogues, whereby the details in the texts, when seen correctly, are both interrelated and intelligibly related to the doctrines (*Lehren*) contained in Plato's works (8). These remarks afford a glimpse of Schleiermacher's revolutionary conception of Plato: his insistence on working with, and correcting misunderstandings of, the written dialogues themselves; his deep belief in the (inapparent) unity—the (nonobvious) interconnectedness—of thought and presentation in the dialogues; and his conviction that a systematic and unified Platonic philosophy, including Plato's doctrines, pervades all of the dialogues, with each individual proposition being inextricable from its context in the text.[5] Along with its devotion to a philosophical system, Schleiermacher's approach to Plato's form is notably literary in its nonlinear and comprehensive attention to the whole text.

In explaining his criteria for identifying authentic works of Plato, rather than those spuriously attributed to him, Schleiermacher insists on Plato's commitment to "this peculiar form" (*diese eigentümliche Form*), an "art" (*Kunst*) of writing that Plato uses to address all topics great and small (36–37).[6] The following sentence gives a fuller description of the form's peculiarities:

> To the inward and essential condition of the Platonic form belongs everything in the composition resulting from the purpose of

---

[4] Much of the "General Introduction" may be read as a rather direct response to Tennemann. So Krämer 1990:222n34, Szlezák 1997:51–53, Lamm 2000:218–222.

[5] On context, see Schleiermacher 1836:14 and Krämer 1990:219n4. Nails 1995:36–43 identifies a modern version of "literary-contextualism" that counterbalances the "analysis" associated with analytic philosophy.

[6] Note the similarity between Tennemann's question ("*Warum wählte Plato gerade diese Form ... ?*"), Schleiermacher's reference to "*diese eigentümliche Form*," and Blondell's twenty-first-century version "Why, then, did Plato choose to write philosophy in this peculiar form?" (2002:38).

compelling the mind of the reader to spontaneous production of ideas: that frequent recommencement of the investigation from another point of view, provided nevertheless that all these threads do actually unite in a common center-point; that progression, often in appearance capricious , and only excusable from the loose tenor which a dialogue might have, but which nevertheless is always purposeful and artful; further, the concealment of the greater goal under a lesser one; the indirect commencement with some individual instance; the dialectic play with ideas, under which, however, the relation to the whole and to the original ideas is continually progressing: these are the conditions some of which must necessarily be found in all really Platonic works that have any philosophical bearing.

37–38

Schleiermacher does not deny that the dialogue form goes all over the place, but neither does he view this waywardness as a regrettable distraction. Instead, he tells us that the written composition (the whole as a specific ordering of its specific parts) is entirely motivated by a firm "purpose" (*Absicht*), which is to "compel" (*nötigen*) readers to think for themselves.[7] The successful reader of Plato knows how to discern "the great purposefulness in the composition of his writings" (*die große Absichtlichkeit in der Zusammensetzung seiner Schriften*, 5). Although Schleiermacher clearly holds that form and content in the dialogues are "inseparable" (*unzertrennlich*, 14), his account resembles Tennemann's in the way it must separate irrelevant appearance from purposeful reality. This separation is especially strong in Schleiermacher's description of the "concealment" (*Verbergen*) whereby a meaningful but inapparent current of activity is located "under" the surface.[8] Indeed, elsewhere in the "General Introduction," Schleiermacher tries to convince those readers who turn toward extratextual sources for the philosophy they are unable to find in the writings that Plato's philosophy is a kind of "product" (*Ausbeute*) that can demonstrably be "taken from" (*entnommen*) the writings (13). This metaphor, redolent of mining for valuable ore, would seem more suited to the traditional extraction of doctrines than a holistic attentiveness to local contexts.

In his eagerness to affirm the unity of Platonic thought, Schleiermacher echoes Tennemann's focus on "the authentic topic" (*den eigentlichen Gegenstand*) when he refers to "the authentic content" (*den eigentlichen Inhalt*) of the

---

[7] Cf. Schleiermacher 1836:14. Cooper 1997 provides a modern example of this common sentiment: a dialogue's literary form helps make it a "springboard for our own further philosophical thought" (xxii).

[8] Cf. Szlezák 1999:12–17 on concealment.

dialogues, "which is rarely expressed literally" (7). Yet although the nature and location of this content are ambiguous, in part because of ordinary and inevitable terminological metaphors, the implications of Schleiermacher's model have been significant. Schleiermacher explains that one can retrieve a system of doctrines gradually, by accounting for details in their contexts and by gaining a proper perspective on the whole.[9] At the same time, he may be said to place a systematic philosophical purpose between the reader and the philosophical system; thus greater goals (but not necessarily doctrines themselves) are concealed under seemingly incidental preoccupations, and unity underlies manifest contradiction. To some extent, that is, Schleiermacher's unity comes not from a univocal propositional system that is present in any identifiable place in the text, but from a guiding purposefulness that regulates the whole. In this holistic model, local details moving in different directions add up to a directed, systematic whole. For Schleiermacher, a pedagogical, didactic purpose inextricably unifies form and content, and because of that unity, one can progressively extract the philosophy from the writings. In any case, Schleiermacher develops a model of indirect communication in which apparent unruliness, when correctly understood, furthers progress toward a fixed but frequently inapparent educational goal. "So it is requisite that the final object (*das Ende*) of the investigation be not directly enunciated and put down in words"; readers, according to Schleiermacher, are not allowed to "rest content ... in possession of the final result [*das Ende*]" without having first been "led on the way [*Weg*]" (17). Here, Plato's gradual and devious promotion of his philosophy substitutes for straightforward and immediate didacticism. For many scholars today, this view has become a model of rhetoric, which I will discuss at length below: Plato is making effective use of literary language in order to pursue a didactic philosophical agenda. Because this view relies on an understanding of Plato's goal or purpose in order to explain why Plato used the dialogue form, I will call this a *teleological* response to the question of literary form.

Whereas Tennemann refers to systematic results that are decorated or concealed by a charming manner of writing, Schleiermacher's "General Introduction" gives more credence to a great paradox of Platonic-Socratic education: the teacher does not directly hand over the goods. Ideally, the Socratic teacher (who has a heightened awareness of ignorance) guides the student to look for the truth. But how exactly is this guidance to be provided in writing; how could a pedagogical purpose itself be a proxy "content" leading necessarily, compellingly toward the author's teachings? Without a commodity

---

[9] As described by Krämer 1990, Schleiermacher holds that Plato's system "unfolds in successive stages, according to a precise didactic plan" (3–4).

to hand over, Plato is teaching students to pursue a method that presumedly only leads where it is supposed to go: to Platonism. The problem can be put in stark terms: how do you get from an overtly unruly text to a univocal, systematic teaching? According to Schleiermacher's model of indirect communication, Plato the writer withholds what he knows, and the notion of content (what we want to get *from* the text) is therefore shifted from an immediate content to a postponed telos—the goal is not to retrieve a doctrine contained in the text, but to follow the text toward an end result.[10]

The text is a means to that end. But getting from overt waywardness to covert purposefulness by way of the text remains a profound difficulty for the interpretation of interconnected form and content in Plato. Recognizing Schleiermacher as a forerunner in the modern shift of attention to Plato's dialogue form, Thomas Szlezák writes that the recent focus "has remained mainly lip-service; the unity of content and form, announced so programmatically, has rarely had any concrete consequences for interpreting Plato" (1999:85).[11] While acknowledging that significant efforts continue to be made, I agree with Szlezák on this point, but for a reason very different from his. For Szlezák, Schleiermacher initiated a "naïve belief" in "the art of 'indirect' communication" (79) that expects far more from writing than Plato ever did— Szlezák insists that the texts we have by Plato must be supplemented by specific oral teachings so that we may grasp the authentic philosophy. My criticism of Schleiermacher's legacy in this chapter concerns the untenable combination of literary hermeneutics with philosophical goals. In my view, Plato's writing obtrusively mediates his thought, and this mediation opens a distance that is by no means easy to cross or eliminate, however much sensitive and sophisticated readers may wish to overcome differences between form and content, or between literature and philosophy. It is tempting to argue that the distance is merely apparent; but as long as one holds that the appearance of the text is indeed significant rather than merely formal or merely literary, how can that

---

[10]   For Szlezák, however, the text points outside itself, to other texts and ultimately to oral doctrines that have left traces but no longer exist. Szlezák's view is first and foremost a historical attempt to recover what Plato meant to teach only to those ready to learn it. His argument relies heavily on the *Phaedrus*, the *Seventh Letter*, and "the historical reality of a doctrine of principles which was never set down in writing—the doctrine of principles which Aristotle prefers to cite in his criticism of Plato in the *Metaphysics*" (1999:31). See also Szlezák 1985. I will suggest below that this sort of historical project, while perfectly valid in itself, is categorically different from reading the dialogues as texts in their own right. Cf. Krämer's conviction that "the sphere of the esoterica" needs to be "elevated to a concrete historical reality comparable to the writings" (1990:12). To the degree that the esoterica do not exist in writing, I must insist that, once elevated, their concrete reality would be incomparably different from that of writings that actually do exist.

[11]   Cf. Klein 1965:3–10.

distance be merely apparent? Once the form of a Platonic dialogue meets with consistent and comprehensive analysis, the distance between Plato's writing and his thinking can no longer appear to vanish into content alone.

Looking for Content Beyond Form

When approaching the surge of interest in Plato's written artistry, it may also be instructive to review attitudes expressed by René Schaerer, along with those of Szlezák, in the twentieth century. Both scholars stress the inadequacy of writing, and they seek to understand and explain how Plato could have meant for his written form to function in a Socratic, philosophical (and Platonic) manner. Crucial to their concerns is the basic contradiction between what Socrates says about the inadequacies of writing (notably in the *Phaedrus* and the *Seventh Letter*) and what Plato does as a writer. But we should also note that this contradiction is but a specific, if particularly reflexive, example of widespread contradictions within and among the dialogues. Thus the inadequacy of writing usually emerges as a twofold problem. First, writing may be inherently inadequate for the project of philosophy. Second, Plato's written dialogues challenge our philosophical methods of reading insofar as statements made in them are sometimes inconsistent; arguments, unruly; positions, abandoned. The things the characters say in the dialogues do not add up neatly; the dialogues are not straightforward. And so it is incumbent on us, according to philosophers such as Schaerer and Szlezák, to develop methods of interpretation that will either avoid or explain away the inadequacies of the written texts and bring us to the elusive philosophical content. Such a focus on philosophical content is a crucial characteristic of philosophical interpretation, strikingly different from the sort of textual focus that I will argue is a hallmark of literary interpretation. Whereas Schleiermacher turns to the texts themselves for a fullness of philosophical meaning, a unity of thought that is inherent in their organic unity of form and content, other interpreters turn beyond the text, eventually finding the form inadequate and looking for the content elsewhere. The views of Schaerer and Szlezák exemplify the strangeness of a focus on form and writtenness or textuality (*Schriftlichkeit*) which, finding the texts inadequate and incomplete in themselves, ends up moving away from written expression in its search for essential content.

Schaerer sharpens Schleiermacher's discussion of interpretation by focusing on "the problem of form" in *La Question platonicienne*, originally published in 1938. He draws a vivid contrast between the sublime simplicity of Platonism and the difficulties posed by Plato's texts: "the written oeuvre is, in many respects, terribly, hopelessly complex: contradictions, obscurities, bizarreries abound" (1969:9; translations mine). Schaerer's approach to the text is conventionally Platonic. Drawing on a Socratic-Platonic theory of Forms, Schaerer says that the subject matter of the dialogues is ultimately the reality of the thing-in-itself (246). "But because this thing is inaccessible to language, it follows that the dialogue finds its point d'appui outside of itself (*en dehors de lui-même*), on a superior plane, and that the rules presiding over its composition are not immanent to it, but transcendent" (246). As a composition based on, and leading toward, a transcendent reality, "the text aspires to be overcome [*dépassé*]" (250). To "overcome" a text is to look beyond it, to treat it as a means or instrument for reaching an "essence" that is "supradiscursive" (247). Hence Plato's "literary oeuvre is only a play of allusions" (251). "One can therefore affirm that Plato wrote nothing, in the sense that one says Socrates knew nothing and said nothing" (251). As a Socratic withholder, Plato the writer is in a sense not a writer; behind, under, or beyond the apparent chaos of our everyday reality of reading lies a transcendent philosophical reality that the reader's vision cannot see on the page.

Where Schaerer is idealistic, Szlezák is primarily historical. Convinced that Plato's written dialogues were complemented by explicit oral teachings, Szlezák writes, "the dialogues are to be read as fragments of Plato's philosophy with a propensity to encourage the reader and at the same time to point beyond themselves. But the form must be regarded as essential for the content" (1999:118). As with Schaerer, the problem of form has been solved by conceiving of the writings as purposefully protreptic—they do not function as a complete expression of the philosophy (the doctrinal content) so much as they turn readers toward it, and thereby lead beyond themselves. And like Schaerer, Szlezák envisages a transcendent process of interpretation: "From the start Plato conceives of philosophical writing ... as writing whose content must be transcended if it is to be fully understood" (1985:66). I take Szlezák to mean that form and content are united in the protreptic usefulness of Plato's texts, but also that this combination of form and content is nevertheless incomplete, not self-sufficient, and not in itself a proper basis for philosophical interpretation.

I certainly do not mean to give the impression that the scholars discussed in this chapter underestimate or neglect Plato's written dialogues. Both Schaerer and Szlezák, more than many, take the dialogue form to be of tremendous importance, as does Schleiermacher. What I wish to highlight is a peculiar methodological phenomenon: modern interest in the *Schriftlichkeit* of the dialogues, driven by a desire to recover Plato's authentic philosophical purposes, tends to adopt an instrumentalist and teleological view of textuality, which paradoxically abandons the written form in favor of a stable Platonic lesson plan. This is so whether the writings are understood to be complete in themselves or parts of a greater undertaking, and whether the lesson is a propositional system of knowledge or a more general call to philosophy. Thus the writings become a meandering path toward something that in Plato's mind was straight. According to this model of interpretation, the indirect appearance of each dialogue belies its underlying didactic directedness.

Bolstered by widespread respect for the evidential power of textual specifics, advances in the treatment of Plato's dialogue form since Schleiermacher have been increasingly influential. Traditional readings, in their disregard for major aspects of the written presentation of Platonic thought, can willfully ignore much of the text itself by sequestering it as peripheral context: who says what in a dialogue, where he says it, and so on. The intellectual historian Gerald Press has been an important chronicler, herald, and advocate for alternative approaches. "An identifiable mode of interpretation of Plato," wrote Press in 1993, referring to the traditional approach, "has prevailed, with rare exceptions, since antiquity" (1993b:107). Press called for greater unity and "self-consciousness" in a "transformation of Plato interpretation that is now taking place" (1993a:viii–ix). This transformation has continued to unfold, leading from a narrow focus on the philosopher's doctrines toward increased attention to features of writing now recognized as literary: features such as characterization, setting, plot, and wordplay. Welcoming the appearance of Debra Nails's Platonic prosopography (Nails 2002), Christopher Rowe signaled "a time when we have come to realise that almost any aspect of a Platonic dialogue may help to throw light on what it is *for*, even, or especially, *philosophically*" (2003:250).[12] From the time when hermeneutic disagreement grew more prominent in the 1980s, however, two sides emerged (with misgivings and unavoidable simplifications) in the academic imagination.[13]

The long-dominant philosophical approach to Plato is one that focuses on logical arguments, propositions, and positions, which it attributes to Plato without much regard for the discursive contexts in which the arguments are presented. While a recent shift in perspective is evident among specialists,

[12] See also Rowe 2007:viii. One may observe a significant change in, e.g., the contrast between Kraut 1992 and 2009, the latter being far more conciliatory toward contextual points of view. (For criticisms of Kraut 1992, see Nails 1995:39–41 and Press 2000:35–37.) Cf. the shift in attitude between Annas 1981 and, say, 1992. Cooper 1997 is notable for using a widely visible forum to emphasize Plato's "renunciation" of authoritative knowledge (xxiii–xxiv). For overviews of literary, dramatic, and contextual approaches, see Klein 1965:3–31; Press 1996, 1998, 2000, and 2012; Nails 1995:36–43.

[13] Nails 1995 describes a "self-destructive duel" characterized by "intense and unhealthy enmity" between two main philosophical approaches; she also notes the potential for disciplinary boundaries (as between philology and philosophy) to complicate such disputes (36). Blondell 2002 laments a "false dichotomy" for which Plato himself is possibly to blame (1), a point to which I will return. See also Gordon 1999:7–13.

the traditional approach—which has been called dogmatic, doctrinal, literalist, analytic, and philosophical—will probably still dominate both the study and especially the teaching of Plato in the foreseeable future. Its orthodoxy is firmly established in, and its authority endorsed by, a powerful current of the Western tradition. The other range of approaches (whose proponents, not surprisingly, have done most of the labeling) has called itself nondogmatic, dialogical, dramatic, literary, and contextualist. The change in perspective owes much to Schleiermacher's holism, although many scholars do not explicitly acknowledge his contribution.[14] By attending to features that are typically identified as literary, the holistic approach contends that Plato's stylistic choices form a context for each proposition he makes in the dialogues, and that this style is therefore essential to any understanding of "what he is trying to say" (McCabe 2008:89). In practice, many scholars continue to combine the two main approaches, insofar as an interest in form need not preclude a search for Plato's doctrines, just as an interest in the unity of form and content need not rule out the unity of Plato's thought.[15] But increased interest in the dialogue form of Plato's writings has shifted the modern gaze in such a way that formal concerns now seem obtrusive and insistent, to the point where they present a glaring challenge to unreflective linear argumentation; and so an exclusive focus on Plato's linear arguments has come to seem limited if not narrow, blinkered, and naïve. My argument here concerns explanations of literary form that conceive of it as goal-driven rhetoric, explanations made by scholars who do in fact take Plato's formal complexity seriously. Although the idea that Plato wrote the way he wrote (rhetorically) in order to say what he wanted to say (univocally) is a neat and nearly indisputable explanation, I see some serious problems in this now-prevalent view of literary form. It bears repeating that for traditionalists focused solely on linear argumentation, a genuine confrontation with the written form of the dialogues can only disappoint, by leading away from univocal, philosophical discourse. Yet for contextual approaches, too, an emphasis on rhetorical persuasion is similarly inadequate to the manifest waywardness of Plato's texts. As long as the asystematic texture of Plato's dialogues is surrendered to the retrieval or reconstruction of a persuasive agenda (inevitably tantamount to a didactic system), rhetoric will always remain a set of superficial devices, separable from a presumptive substance.

---

[14] Press is a notable exception.

[15] E.g. Kahn 1996 and Rowe 2007 value both context and doctrine, taking different views of Plato's possible development as a thinker over the course of different dialogues, and claiming to account for literary style while reading in what is, as I argue below, a decidedly philosophical (i.e. nonliterary) manner.

The Status of the Dialogues:
Did Plato Write Platonic Dialogues?

Given how little we actually know about Plato's own view of the dialogue form, we could turn to a writer like Shakespeare for a momentary comparison. Does it even make sense to ask after Shakespeare's motive for writing *Hamlet* as a play rather than a treatise? And what is the goal of *Hamlet*? Is the *form* of *Hamlet* merely ornamental, merely aesthetic, merely literary? Plato's dialogues are certainly not Shakespearean plays—and Shakespeare was not what we call a philosopher—but contrary to popular belief, we do not know how Plato intended his writings to function, and the practice of philosophy itself has gone in directions that he could not have foreseen. Meanwhile, asking why Plato wrote in the way he did rests heavily on the assumption that Plato's text is always teaching us a lesson of some sort. Even simply to question this assumption is unorthodox. Many experts find the notion of a nondidactic Plato inconceivable, but their sincere conviction on this point should not foreclose all further investigation.[16] In any case, it is worth noting that a prejudicial certainty about Plato's goals can create an undesirable methodological tautology: it may limit interpretation to finding what was already presumed to be there, what we always expected to find—the moral of the story, if you will: the lesson of Platonic philosophy waiting as a foregone conclusion. Uncooperative features of the text are thus destined to be ironed out (justified, straightened) after the fact.

Without a doubt, Plato was one of the world's greatest thinkers and teachers. Even if we could bracket Plato's intellectual-historical influence (and lose the benefit to humanity from having read him), a nondidactic Plato would be difficult even to imagine.[17] It is nevertheless worthwhile to consider how the inherited view of Plato's purposes underpins the modern (and ancient) reading of his texts. As noted above, the problem of literary form has been addressed in modern times by way of questions that lead back to Plato's philosophical motivations: "Why did Plato write *dialogues*?" asks one scholar; "Why so much deviousness on Plato's part?" asks another, who wonders about "Plato's motive for

---

[16] Press 1993a:viii suggests that questioning whether Plato's dialogues "are meant to communicate any settled teachings" is a key focus for the "new Platonism." Questioning Plato's didacticism per se has proved unpalatable for most mainstream researchers. See also Scott 2007: "Plato must have wanted to communicate something in some way. But in what way do dramatic works 'communicate'?" (xix). And if one starts to ask how works of art communicate, didactically is not the only answer.

[17] Note Press's distinction between Platonism and "the study and interpretation of the dialogues in and for themselves" (1998:309). In this sense, Platonic philosophy—like professional philosophy itself, for that matter—is a historical development focused on the thought of a historical figure rather than a text-oriented interpretation of Plato's writings.

holding back"; "Why, then," writes a third, "did Plato choose to write philosophy in this peculiar form?"[18] These questions express an admirable unwillingness to ignore the particularity of the texts as Plato wrote them. But they also presume that these texts are peculiar by way of contrast with a philosophical norm, a blend of philosophy and discourse that was not firmly established until after Plato's time. Plato did not write what we expect him to have written: namely, univocal philosophical treatises. According to Northrop Frye's handy definition of philosophical discourse, "philosophy is assertive or propositional writing" (1957:329), and it is against this background that Plato's way of writing stands out.[19] Frye's remark captures two relevant aspects of philosophy, understood as a genre or discourse type. For one thing, proper philosophical discourse (so understood) states points, and it does so avowedly. This philosophy is linear and rational argumentation, taking us from point A to point B along a straightforward path of reasoning that should not rely on turns of phrase. As is often noted, Plato did not write like Aristotle (even if Aristotle did sometimes write like Plato, in now-lost dialogues, and even if Aristotle treated Plato's writings like treatises). Compared with the syllogistic progression of Aristotelian discourse, Plato's style is certainly peculiar. Frye's formulation also suggests that philosophy is essentially a practice of writing. Lectures, conversations, and solitary thinking are, at best, profound but ephemeral philosophical activities, which may enter the genre of philosophy itself only through written discourse. (And Socrates is a paradoxical catalyst of the Western tradition, known only from a distance, not by his writing but by having been written about.) In any case, by focusing on the dialogue form as the context of Platonic philosophy, readers are apt to continue seeking a univocal text (philosophical content) hidden inside a dialogical context (literary form).

As a piece of writing, each dialogue is a verbal mechanism that arguably presents readers with more perplexities than instructions. "When one compares Plato with some of the other philosophers who are often ranked with him—Aristotle, Aquinas, and Kant, for example—he can be recognized to be far more exploratory, incompletely systematic, elusive, and playful than they" (Kraut 2009:3). Strangely enough, even though Plato's writings largely underlie our conception of philosophy, our conception calls for sustained, direct, and coherent argumentation, a mode of communication that is often manifestly

---

[18] Griswold 2002:143, Kahn 1996:65, Blondell 2002:38. Kahn acknowledges (65–66) that a writer's manner is likely to have many motivations; Rutherford 1995 makes a similar point (8–10).

[19] Like any genre, this one has seen any number of exceptions and challenges; nevertheless, the category of straightforward, reasoned argumentation in expository prose does exist as a norm and has had a far greater historical impact on the interpretation of Plato than, say, the niche into which we might fit Kierkegaard or Nietzsche, whom we see more as modern subverters of expository norms than as inheritors of Plato's ancient subversiveness.

abandoned or perverted in the dialogues themselves. Yet most readers, even those who acknowledge the texture of the dialogues, begin with an institutionalized assumption that has far-reaching effects: Plato is presumed to have designed each text to lead us toward a foreknown goal, to lead us to some brand of Platonism. This assumption comes naturally when we move from Plato the legendary thinker to Plato the writer. Plato was a philosopher; therefore, what he wrote must have been in the service of philosophy. Plato was a teacher and continues to be our teacher; therefore, Plato's texts are, to put it crudely, teaching machines.[20] Where are we to find Plato's real thought if not in his writings?[21] His writings, one presumes, must have been made—and must be made—to communicate his real teachings, his fixed beliefs.[22] It is the *must be made*, the active pressure on interpretation that I see being imposed by our preconceptions about philosophy, that gives me some pause about this conventional line of reasoning. And this pressure is one of the driving forces behind the conception of literary form as rhetoric, and of rhetoric as persuasion in the service of philosophy.

So literary form emerges as a problem largely because of our expectations. We want to have a Plato of propositions and assertions, but instead we have a diverse collection of perspectivized propositions and assertions. The corollary implied in questions about the dialogue form is this: Why did Plato manifestly not write *expository* discourse? That is, why did he not manifestly urge something (whether some kind of convincing wisdom or a wise course of action) on his readers? With a seemingly minor change in emphasis, one comes to ask why Plato did not write *manifestly* expository discourse. Either way, the presumption that Plato was a didactic writer leads to an answer something like this: Plato did not write manifestly didactic discourse because he wrote covertly didactic discourse. On the one hand, the dialogues seem to taunt us with the prospect of wisdom and guidance withheld. Regardless of his motives, Plato's choice of literary form suggests to many that he hid his real meaning in the dialogues as in puzzles to be solved by readers.[23] On the other hand, Plato's

---

[20] Press 1997:3 traces a similar line of assumptions underlying dogmatic interpretations of the dialogues: "since Plato is a philosopher, he must have doctrines." My emphasis here is less on doctrines per se than on *teachings* as a presumptive notion that, while perhaps nondogmatic, continues to guide or control the process of interpretation.

[21] Again, the possibility of an unpublished but doctrinal legacy only underscores my point that a historical focus on Plato's *thinking* is likely to lead away from his *writing*.

[22] Schleiermacher: "it is clear that he must (*er muß*) have endeavored to make written instruction as like as possible to that better [Socratic] kind, and he must (*es muß ihm*) also have succeeded" (1836:16). See also Cohn 1999:27 on what John Updike called the "must have" school of speculative biography.

[23] So Kraut, quoted above. Cf. Scott 2007: "The more one studies Plato's dialogues, the more one has the gathering sense that Plato 'knows' more than he reveals in his works" (xviii). Hence

15

dialogues are saturated with explicit arguments. But the abundance of argumentation embedded in the dialogues only heightens the taunting quality that readers notice when they try to extrapolate a point from their written form. For contextual readers who do not presume that a dialogue will have a dogmatic agenda, an explicit argument in the context of a conversation or a speech will always be significantly different from a straightforward, authoritative, expository declaration.

Having expected expository treatises from Plato and being faced with overtly digressive dialogues, scholars naturally turn to conventional generic categories in order to determine the Platonic text's status or type of discourse, and the author's stance or intention. The status might be, among other possibilities, fictional, historical, dramatic, theoretical, philosophical, literary, or experimental. The stance could be, for example, didactic, dogmatic, skeptical, playful, proleptic, propaedeutic, or provisional. Unfortunately, such overlapping terms potentially introduce new confusions, and the theoretical problems involved are extraordinarily difficult. But even more confounding: Plato and his contemporaries were exploring and developing the conventions of genre and discourse that we now take for granted in the Western tradition; it furthermore seems clear that Plato was transgressing the generic boundaries recognized even in his time; and there is no reliable account of Plato's stated intentions. Can we presume to know the final cause, the telos of Plato's written dialogues; that is, why Plato wrote dialogues and not treatises? The telos is usually assumed to be some combination of education and Platonic philosophy. The teleological approach to Plato is in accord with a long-established goal of philosophy in general: to reconstruct what Plato thought and what he wanted to teach us. Indeed, this goal or telos is essential to philosophy's own self-understanding as a pursuit that follows in Plato's footsteps.[24] The possession of this goal (tantamount to a desired commodity that Plato possessed) has led analytically minded interpreters to ignore dialogical contexts of argumentation at will, and has led literary-minded interpreters to explain Plato's form and wording in terms of a

---

the persistent efforts of readers—encouraged, one may well argue, by the texts themselves—to reach through the works toward a commodity that seemingly ought to be have been prepossessed by Plato and then put into them. Consider this biographical anecdote testifying to Plato's legendary, taunting elusiveness: just before his death, Plato dreamed of turning into a swan, "and leaping from tree to tree, he frustrated the attempts of the bird-catchers to hunt him down" (Olympiodorus *Commentary on Plato's Alcibiades*, Riginos 1976:24). Annas 1996 also emphasizes Plato's elusiveness.

[24] If "the dialogues are supposed to teach us a philosophical lesson"—which is thus identified as an assumption—then the first lesson Plato taught us, notes M. Frede with a nod to Whitehead, is how to write "footnotes to Plato" (Frede 1992:219).

rhetorically purposeful, didactic master plan. In both instances, it appears that our goal has been aligned with Plato's goal.

We do know that the genre of Socratic discourses was a specific precedent for Plato's type of dialogue, and it is likely that Plato was sometimes emulating or playing off against contemporary writers.[25] At the same time, as pointed out by Andrea Nightingale, Plato brings the conventions of multiple genres (such as tragedy, epic, oratory, and history) into dialogue with each other, thereby differentiating and advancing his own brand of philosophical activity.[26] Insofar as Plato is "introducing and defining a radically different discursive practice" against a backdrop of ancient conventions, the historical context cannot help us much with the unconventional status of his texts—unless his once-radical version of philosophy actually is in accord with our now-familiar version.[27] Otherwise, we are still left trying to reconstruct or establish some ground rules for interpreting a radically challenging corpus. Even if Plato may be said to have invented philosophy—as Nightingale proposes, while acknowledging concerns about the tendency to retroject our version of philosophy back into its origins— the texts he left us are not what the subsequent tradition of philosophy would lead us to expect.[28] All of which suggests that the invention was and remains unconventional. R. B. Rutherford sums up the situation acutely: "Neither the origins nor the generic status of the dialogue form can be firmly established: in the one case this is a matter of lost evidence, in the other it reflects the genuine complexity of Plato's literary enterprise."[29]

Nor does the historical reception of Plato's writings offer a helpful vantage point from which to assess the author's stance or the texts' status. The difficulties in interpreting Plato's writings have always been there—and whether or not his dialogues were designed to do so, they have provoked an extraordinarily varied and industrious response. In a general introduction to ancient philosophy, Julia Annas adduces the *Republic* as a prime example of why we should not take our current assessment of ancient works for granted, citing basic facts of history that are little known by the public and rarely allowed to interfere with modern interpretation. "Plato is the only author for whom we can feel certain that we possess all the works he made public.... But even Plato is not a straightforward author to read; for one thing, the dialogue form distances the author from the ideas he puts forward, and interpretations of Plato are probably the most

---

[25]   See Rutherford 1995:10–15; Kahn 1996:1–35; Nightingale 1995; Ford 2010.

[26]   Nightingale 1995:1–12. I simultaneously agree with Rutherford: "The Platonic dialogue is too familiar, too central to the classical tradition, for us to realize how remarkable it must have seemed at first" (1995:15).

[27]   The quotation (if not necessarily the point) comes from Nightingale 1995:5, with 10nn30–31.

[28]   Nightingale 1995:10–11, with reference to Kraut 1992:1. Cf. Annas 2000:19–36.

[29]   Rutherford 1995:15. Cf. Press 1997:7–12.

varied of any ancient philosopher" (2000:23). Annas summarizes "the changing fortunes" of the *Republic*: while today this dialogue holds a dominant position in the canon of ancient philosophy, for centuries it attracted far less attention, and was rarely celebrated for its Idealist metaphysics or its ideal model of political organization, which were eventually favored and promoted by Benjamin Jowett and others starting in the nineteenth century.[30] "Throughout the seventeenth and eighteenth centuries," notes Annas, "Plato fell into philosophical neglect, and the *Republic* was regarded as a mere oddity, if it was regarded at all" (27–28). Thus the reception of Plato's dialogues (and of the *Republic*, whose history offers a particularly striking example of vicissitudes in reception) is unlikely to contribute decisive evidence as to the generic, discursive, and pragmatic intentions or motives of its author. Historical data concerning reception can certainly inform our ways of thinking about the dialogues: "The ancient Platonists," for instance, "remind us of how Plato was read in the ancient world—that is, for some hundreds of years; and this may at the very least give us some perspective on our own assumptions in reading Plato."[31] And the historical data will, one hopes, keep growing in depth and accuracy. But ultimately, Plato's contemporaries and immediate followers were no more straight on this than we are— these resources give vital insight into the historical development of Platonic philosophy, but when it comes to the historical-biographical fact of Plato's stance as a writer of dialogues, they are nothing more or less than more speculation. The study of ancient texts would get nowhere without such speculation, but the "overwhelming impression" that Plato wrote to teach us lessons should not blind us to our methodological limitations.[32]

---

[30] Annas 2000:19–36. For a different perspective, see Pappas 2013:273–282. See also Press 1996 for a more detailed discussion of reception and the *Republic*. Press 1996:72n16 and Ferrari 2007:510 list relevant secondary literature on the topic.

[31] Annas 1999:2. Writing of the development from Socratic to Platonic ethics, Annas also suggests that the "framework for reading, teaching, and discussing Plato is so familiar that it may come to seem inescapable. It is a presupposition of discussion rather than something to be discussed itself" (4).

[32] For the "overwhelming impression," see Cooper 1997:xxv.

2

Philosophical Rhetoric

IN A REEXAMINATION OF THE METHODOLOGICAL LIMITATIONS just introduced, this chapter poses a fundamental opposition between expository
and literary paradigms of interpretation. I will begin by distinguishing several
methods of interpretation by discipline and by their attitudes toward history,
on the grounds that historical inquiry's methodological focus on information
(which we have already glimpsed in Szlezák's subordination of Plato's written
texts to a historical recovery of what Plato really thought) may help to clarify
the difference between expository and literary outlooks. Then I will consider
a related disciplinary divide between ancient and modern conceptions of
rhetoric. It is worthwhile, I have found, to view both of these as hermeneutic
conceptions, distinguishable along expository–literary lines. Whereas an interpretation that follows the ancient model of rhetoric undertakes an expository
mission of historical recovery, modern literary analysis adopts a model of rhetoric that leads to the exploration of themes as opposed to theses. The vocabulary
of scholarship in this area of textual hermeneutics frequently lacks adequate
precision, especially when it is shared by different disciplines; moreover, the
study of Plato's dialogues raises an inexhaustible array of problems. I therefore
offer a broad, schematic, and viable framework that encompasses some recog-
nizable assumptions and some general working terms for shared consideration.

As should become clear, I am less immediately interested in the status
of Plato's writing per se (whether it is literary or philosophical or both, for
instance) than in the conceptual premises held by different groups of interpreters.[1] At bottom, these methodologies reflect how readers use the text—how
they want it to function and what they expect to find and experience when
reading it. Various academic disciplines have presumably honed their methods
in order to meet their different goals and expectations. Rather than dwell
on quarrels over literary and philosophical objects of study, one can address

---

[1]   Cf. Culler 2007: "For many works, it does not seem to be objective properties that make them
    literature but rather the fact that they are read in certain ways, placed in the cultural framework
    of literature, subject to particular sorts of attention" (229).

the problem of literary form in Plato by identifying certain key choices and assumptions that interpreters typically make in order to pursue their respective "purposes and interests."[2] My main suggestion here is that we provisionally recognize and maintain a consistent rather than a haphazard distinction between literary and expository conceptions of reading. In this schema, literary approaches are oriented toward the composition of the text itself as the primary object of study, and their claims concern the text as created by the author. Expository approaches, in contrast, look through the text toward univocal messages installed in it by the author, messages that readers can extract and then consider separately from the wording of the written composition. Each choice of focus has its uses, and in practice interpreters do many different (and sometimes contradictory) things simultaneously with texts. I am neither proposing prescriptive categories nor recommending any one choice over any other. As I see it, however, an implicit difference between literary and expository methods already informs most interpretation. Academic interpreters in all disciplines recognize, to put it one way, "a permanent 'bar' of difference between the *figural* language of creative literature and the *referential* language of scientific or philosophical discourse."[3] Yet in interpreting Plato, this normal boundary is frequently and misleadingly crossed. Generally speaking, principles of literary interpretation clash with expository desires in even self-avowedly literary interpretations of Plato; and traditional, doctrinal interpretations of the dialogues remain patently expository.

So I begin by elaborating on three relevant kinds of textual interpretation: textual criticism (which establishes the text), literary criticism or analysis (which views the established text as a composition), and philosophical interpretation (which uses the established text to contemplate the author's univocal thinking). "Classics," suggests Lowell Edmunds, "makes a distinction between interpretation or literary criticism, on the one hand, and philology, on the other, of which textual editions and commentaries are the *chefs d'oeuvre*" (2005:8). I am unsure whether Edmunds's statement accurately describes the current state of classical studies, but I consider the distinction a valid and helpful one to make. It is easily lost because the discipline of classical studies as a whole (including its literary-critical branch) has long-standing and indispensible historical interests. In any case, the basic idea is that textual scholarship establishes an authoritative text, whereas literary criticism interprets the established text. Yet the

---

[2]   Stout 1982; I follow Heath 2002 in drawing on Stout's view of meaning in interpretation. Cf. Marshall 1992: "interpreters decide, on the basis of their own interests and questions, what materials to interpret and what practices will satisfy the need or desire to interpret them" (162).

[3]   Greetham 1999:345, describing efforts by poststructuralist writers to subvert this bar. See also Frye 1957:5, 86.

crucial distinction is not between natural science and humanistic interpretation; textual scholarship, as a matter of course, must make many interpretive judgments as well as technical decisions.[4] Instead, a crucial difference between these two methods of interpreting texts may be found in their interests and purposes. As a rule, the textual critic is theoretically oriented toward the past and has no wish to go beyond boundaries imposed by the past, regardless of the reconstructive criteria adopted. Thus the critic gives priority to earlier objects, events, and ideas in order to prepare a text for other, later types of interpretation. (Even radical textual critics who treat the text as a social construction rather than the author's intended creation are still reconstructing the history of its construction.) A critical edition is thus presented as a methodical interpretation of historical phenomena. And the text is in one sense an end in itself: fixation is itself the primary goal of the text-critical interpretation, and the fixed text is a body of data that can be used as readers see fit.

Thus conceived, a written text is a fixed ordering of specific words: "a text is any discourse fixed by writing" (Ricoeur 1981:145). *Discourse* here refers to a specific and communicative passage of language that is longer than a sentence, and types of discourse are categories of usage associated with different situations in which language is used to communicate; as in historical, philosophical, or literary discourse. What I wish to stress first is that every written text is *fixed* and that this fixedness sets a standard for the composition's authority, giving us an evidential basis for subsequent interpretation. (A text may be fixed repeatedly, at various points in its life, giving us different editions or incarnations.) In a particular case such as the *Republic*, specific choices, ideally those made by Plato in his deployment of words, have been fixed as a unique composition. In their historical reconstructions of the text, experts (epigraphers, papyrologists, paleographers, textual critics, and so on) have pursued an ideal of factual accuracy.[5] For each text-critical question, there can in principle only be one correct answer, and the answer concerns an ideal object of desire that is conceived as a preexisting artifact.[6] Editorial questions concerning the fixed

---

4   Greetham 1994: "The single most important characteristic of textual *criticism* (that part of textual scholarship charged with interrogating the text and preparing it for public consumption, usually in the form of a scholarly edition) is that it is *critical*, it does involve speculative, personal, and individual confrontation of one mind by another, despite the attempts by some textual critics to turn the process into a science" (295).

5   Here I differ from Heath 2002:86, who does not see a separation of editorial from interpretive practices in classical studies.

6   Experts also sometimes choose to reconstruct multiple texts under a single traditional designation, and they may recognize the involvement of multiple authorial minds as well as hands in the formulation of artifacts. See Nagy 2004:25–39 for an evolutionary model of textualization in the oral tradition of Homeric poetry. Variorum and multiple-text editions of plays by Shakespeare are prominent examples of a similar kind.

text itself regularly arise when interpreting classical texts, but these questions are addressed (again, in principle) with the distinct techniques of textual criticism, even when textual critic and literary critic are one and the same philologist. The specific form of a Greek text such as the *Republic*, presumed to have been determined by the author, assumes its place as a stable sequence of words that can be copied repeatedly, cited accurately, and described from different perspectives by different readers without losing its integrity. As it happens, all of Plato's major writings seem to have survived, and they are in relatively good shape, with Slings's Oxford Classical Text edition of 2003 bringing the *Republic* into the twenty-first century.

So textual criticism is a specialized kind of interpretation, working in any genre (literary or expository, traditional or radical) but giving theoretical priority to historical evidence. The reconstruction of an ideal text thereby results in a real and fixed text. With different goals in mind, the literary critic (by which I mean an interpretive analyst of texts) uses the fixed text as evidence about itself; how it articulates ideas, how its patterns create emphasis.[7] Thus the literary interpreter reflects on the text, in an intellectual conversation where reader and text mutually reinforce emerging perspectives. The views of the composition that emerge from this procedure as scholarly claims are essentially *about* the text. Certainly—and this should be stressed to avoid misunderstanding— the literary critic is no more divorced from history than from expository comprehension. (Indeed, many branches of literary and cultural studies have a fundamentally historical orientation.[8]) The point here is that while a literary analysis of a text must adduce evidence from many contexts (historical, cultural, and so on), the text necessarily remains the central node where all contexts meet, and from which their relevance emanates. Otherwise, the result is a different sort of analysis. Once we accept Plato's *Republic* as a fixed composition and an existing cultural monument, it has an inexorable integrity. The text is a specific arrangement of specific words, and this web of linguistic complexity is the *texture* of the composition. Literary scholars (whom I must here insist on distinguishing from, among others, editors, who have different goals in mind) would no sooner rewrite parts of Plato's text than repaint a stroke of color in a portrait by van Gogh. Indeed, the *Republic*'s specificity is not only essential to its

---

[7] Cf. Culler 1988: "One of the signal virtues of literary criticism is that it does not deem its texts to be simply data about something else" (278).

[8] The literary historian has still another goal: using the text (along with any other relevant information) as evidence to make historical claims. This is how I understand Heath's historically oriented, intentionalist model of interpretation: Heath's ideal is to make historical (expository) determinations rather than explore perspectives afforded by the text (2002). While I embrace Heath's pragmatic model of pluralism, I consider his recommended method of interpretation to be not literary but historical in orientation.

existence as a shared cultural artifact but is, as Schleiermacher recognized, also the web of evidence on which any interpretation must rest (if it is, in fact, to be an interpretation of the text as an integral composition). So it is axiomatic that literary interpretation focuses on "meaning that is indissociable from the structure of a particular text" (Marshall 1992:171). My emphasis on the text's specificity may seem unnecessarily labored, especially in light of the careful scrutiny regularly accorded to ancient texts—to the structure and the philosophical terminology of the *Republic*, for instance—but it is precisely the significance of the specifics, as organized in dialogue form, that is at issue here. As for contexts, these are countless, but the most urgent context in every instance of literary analysis is the specific text itself, understood as a composition whose elements are interrelated components of an integral whole, rather than independent and easily excised pieces of a mosaic.[9]

Besides textual criticism and literary interpretation, we must now take into account another way that scholars pursue textual analysis: philosophical interpretation. The practice of philosophy is broad and diverse, and when it comes to studying Plato, a variety of priorities emerge. Philosophers read Plato in order to comprehend logical arguments, which are paraphrasable lines of reasoning, propositions, and assertions found in the dialogues; to reconstruct the beliefs, claims, and teachings of Plato (and of many other individual thinkers, most especially Socrates); and to test or debate the logic of arguments and claims, both on their own terms and in light of subsequent argumentation. Each of these three tasks is important in its own right, and virtually any academic philosopher, whether inclined to a monological or a dialogical approach to Plato, would recognize their validity. For the current discussion, I set aside the third (which evaluates the general truth or validity of particular arguments) as an exercise in logical reasoning rather than textual interpretation per se; yet in some ways, paradoxically, this logical and abstract sort of analysis most closely resembles interpretation, insofar as both engage in an ongoing exploration of questions and problems. The other two goals, comprehension and reconstruction, assume that some fixed version of Plato's thought is waiting to be grasped. And here, as with textual criticism, I see an essentially historical project. So part of what I am saying—if we leave aside the contemporary exploration of truth, wisdom, and logic—is simply this: the philosophical interpretation of Plato's texts is a project in the history of philosophy.[10] And, I would add, the history of philosophy is a

---

9   The importance of taking a Platonic dialogue as a whole is emphasized by, among others, McCabe 2008:89, Blondell 2002:4–5, Cooper 1997:xxiii, Press 1993b.

10   Kahn 2000, for example, sees issues of chronology as highly relevant to the interpretation of Plato's dialogues because "chronology is the backbone of any historical understanding" (190), which includes the history of philosophy. But Kahn is not suggesting, as I am, that history is the

philosopher-centric discipline: Plato's thought is the goal and Plato's writings are usually considered the best available means to that goal.

It may be troubling here to suggest that the philosophical interpretation of Plato's dialogues has a biographical goal (to know what Plato himself actually believed) and that the text is, as a matter of course, an instrumental fund of evidence in a resolutely intentionalist project. In other words, the text is an important instrument for undertaking this task, but an instrument nonetheless. If textual criticism's historical claims concerning ancient texts are fraught with conjecture and speculation, the philosophical attempt to recover what ancient thinkers thought, insofar as it posits what was going on in a human being's mind, might appear to be a quixotic attempt at mind reading. And for this reason, it may appear that I am trying somehow to belittle this project, when I wish instead to recognize its premises and delineate its scope. In fact, studying the history of philosophy involves a perfectly ordinary and respectable—and indispensably practical—kind of historical intentionalism. The author's written communication is taken to contain and convey information that we strive to receive and comprehend accurately. In other words, philosophical texts as such are taken to be *expository*. This is an accepted assumption in academia, as in less deliberate settings. Nor is this intentionalism an affront to the literary-critical interrogation of an author's intentions—because the text is not taken to be literary. When practicing modern literary criticism, which is founded precisely on the interdependence of form and content, it makes no sense to look for separable content; by the same token, it makes all the sense in the world for philosophical interpretation to do so. I assume that many philosophers will agree that the philosophical interpretation of texts is indeed something entirely different from literary interpretation. Philosophy is the study of arguments and claims that thinkers have made; and though it usually relies on what they are supposed to have written, this is to interpret their texts for the sake of their arguments, and not the other way around. Accordingly, the distinction poses few problems for the community of orthodox readers who are comfortable ignoring the dialogical "spirit" of Plato's writing, but it spells trouble for those who wish to reach the historical philosopher without bypassing the literary labyrinth of his written compositions. The dilemma is captured in John M. Cooper's advice to readers of Plato. Cooper concedes that the "spirit" in which Plato wrote dialogues makes their interpretation a "dauntingly complex task" (1997:xxiii). While claiming to maintain "full respect" for Plato's renunciation

---

backbone of the philosophical interpretation of Plato generally; in describing his view of Plato's work, Kahn proceeds from a firm "historical claim" about chronology to reach a "hermeneutic hypothesis," which is in turn tested in his interpretation of certain dialogues (190). See also Griswold 1999; Kahn 1996; McPherran 1990.

of authority and his "spirit of experimentation," Cooper also "accepts the overwhelming impression, not just of Antiochus, but of every modern reader of his dialogues, that Platonism nonetheless constitutes a systematic body of 'philosophical doctrine'" (xxv). This latter admission, however, is simply to accept a fact in the history of philosophy—Platonism is, de facto, a systematic body. The difficulty is to reconcile an overwhelmingly accepted impression (Platonism) with the complexity of Plato's profoundly experimental writings.[11]

Literary and Expository Conceptions of Rhetoric

The emphasis on Plato's unwritten doctrines by Krämer, Szlezák, and their cohort suggests a thought experiment. For us today, the historical possibility that Plato in fact made unwritten statements depends on written statements. But rather than try to reconstruct the gist of these doctrines from fragments of hearsay, let us imagine a verifiably authentic and adequately accurate recording of what Plato himself said that he believed. Such a remarkable document would be of tremendous interest to any interpreter of Plato. For the historian of philosophy, the unique value of this imaginary document would come from its being accepted as a univocal, rhetorically transparent presentation of Platonic philosophy, divorced from the tortuous language of the dialogues. We would have the key to understanding the dialogues as philosophy, a key that would compensate for their incomplete or otherwise compromised modes of exposition. For the literary interpreter, however, Plato's dialogues—being integral texts—could never be completed, solved, or opened by the insertion of a separate answer key. The rhetorically transparent version of Plato's beliefs could only solve the expository problems posed by the dialogues; literary problems would revert to the text itself, invigorated but not replaced by new contextual evidence. By the same token, if James Joyce had told us unequivocally, in a certified document, exactly what *Finnegans Wake* meant, how could that document replace *Finnegans Wake*? Only to the extent that we had been looking to the text for evidence of a univocal system of expository messages. Plato and Joyce certainly both communicate their ideas in their writings. But the philosophical

---

[11] Cooper relies on a holistic vision of authorial control to suggest that "it is in the entire writing that the author speaks to us"; so "what the writing itself is saying" equals "what Plato is saying as its author" (1997:xxiii). This appeal to the author's ultimate control threatens to devolve into a truism, flipping Plato's manifest renunciation of authority on its head by confusing authorship with authorial commitment. Blondell 2002:43–45, Rowe 2007:15–16, and Ferrari 2010:28 offer similar explanations, in effect explaining away Plato's glaring absence from his dialogues by implying that any text (if not an entire oeuvre) by a single author must necessarily be treated, in the final analysis, as univocal (i.e. expository).

conception of "what Plato thought" is categorically different from a literary view of "what Joyce thought."

A similar problem arises from the experimental diversity of an author's oeuvre. In the case of Plato's dialogues, "anyone who is interested in Plato's philosophy must find a way to relate the intellectual contents of these works to one another. We cannot ascribe to Plato eighteen different philosophies" (Kahn 1996:37). Although we regularly seek to understand one literary work through reference to others, we would hesitate to ascribe a single, coherent message to all of Catullus' poems, Shakespeare's plays, or Virginia Woolf's novels. All the same, I hope it is clear that my argument here is not a general condemnation of message-seeking intentionalism in interpretation. I am pointing out instead why Plato's rhetoric, when pressed to yield the results desired by the discipline of philosophy, is often reconceived as a collection of crypto-expository, if artful, dodges.

Helen Vendler, a critic of literature in English, offers an unusually lucid account of the expository–literary distinction. Vendler specializes in lyric poetry, and in tandem with her critical writings she has made a strong case for an aesthetic approach to this specific genre. I am not suggesting that we read Plato quite as we might read a poem, play, or novel—the dialogues sprawl over generic borderlines—but that the lyric genre may help to illuminate the relationship between exposition and literary form. On a related note, the term *poetry* often serves in broad categorizations of genre and discourse to indicate the nonexpository status of literature in general—as seen in the German word *Dichtung*, which refers to both poetry and literature generally, and in the traditional notion of *poetics* (as a theory of literature) adopted from Aristotle. Vendler fully recognizes that "criticism may, along the way, make an interpretation or unveil or counter an ideology; but these activities (of paraphrase and polemic) are not criticism of the art work *as* art work, but *as* statement" (1988:1, my emphasis).[12] I draw attention to the word "as" because the reader's approach is a matter of choice—it is not strictly necessitated by a generic form or a type of discourse. My discussion so far should make clear that one ordinarily follows different guiding principles of interpretation when reading a text as history, or as philosophy, or as literature. When reading lyric poetry, where our usual conceptions of form and content are challenged by a condensed use of language, it would be misguided to extract propositions and arguments, and to translate a poem's careful arrangement of words into expository statements and messages. It is nonetheless certainly possible to do so. In fact, it is extraordinarily tempting to look for univocal messages in anything we read.

---

[12] Cf. C. Brooks 1947:192–214; Frye 1957:4–5, 84–85.

Vendler prefers not to speak even of interpreting a lyric poem; interpreters, she says, "fundamentally regard the art work as an allegory: somewhere under the surface (as in a biblical parable) there lies a hidden meaning" that can be trans-literated in expository prose (3). This is quite different from saying that poems are devoid of positions and ideas, but the poetic interest of these ideas is in how they are dynamically refracted in patterns of language.[13] Many readers might think that the job of the literary reader is precisely to look for hidden meanings, yet in Vendler's view, form is nothing other than "content-as-arranged" (3). As long as the reader is looking for a covert ideological content (a content that is usually presumed to hide behind or beneath form), the form will remain a mere vehicle, a disposable veil or shell. Allegorical excavation does not respect the integrity of the text's manifest arrangement of language. "Content disarranged (as in paraphrase) leaves form behind, usually unnoticed" (3). I fully agree with this last point and stress its relevance to the discussion of approaches to Plato, especially approaches that translate Plato's literary form into philosophical discourse by way of rhetoric. We should note, however, that in the metaphorical terminology of textual analysis, disarrangement by paraphrase is also a process of straightening out the various complexities and turnings of linguistic compo-sition, complexities that expository interpretation must ignore in order to reach its univocal goals.[14]

Vendler makes her point about exposition with particular force in the case of Shakespeare's sonnets. "Lyric poetry," she observes, "is almost never assigned in a course on the 'great books' because the exposition of ideas in poetry seems too platitudinous for discussion" (1997b). The main thought of any sonnet, for example, can be expressed in a perfectly straightforward single statement.[15] Still, if Shakespeare is no great statement maker, he is no mean thinker either, and Vendler's aesthetic of the lyric is far from hostile to ideas; the problem is that "the way in which lyric deals with ideas—that is, by trans-forming them into forms—is still incompletely understood" (1997b).[16] What

---

[13] Cf. Vendler 1997a:1–41, esp. 21–25.

[14] See also Aviram 2001.

[15] E.g. Sonnet 30: "Whenever I think about the past, I sink into a melancholy recollection of all my losses; but if, when I am doing this, I think of you, I seem once again to possess all I have lost, and my melancholy ceases" (Vendler 1997b).

[16] Contrast Arieti's experiential aesthetic, which asks that our intellects be satisfied by "lessons" in Plato's dialogues that are true but not "startlingly new," lessons that "do not dazzle with breath-taking novelty" (1998:283). Arieti, who cites Shakespeare, Sophocles, and Euripides as parallels, stands out as an advocate for literary aestheticism in the study of Plato: "The kind of teaching that one receives from art is very different from that which one receives from a philosophical treatise; art works primarily by appealing to our emotions" (283). This strikes me as a dimin-ished and tepid aestheticism, and a poor response to literary form, underestimating the cerebral rewards of a Sophoclean play no less than those of a Platonic dialogue.

we might call poetic thinking exists in the choice and arrangement of words; to extract expository statements from that arrangement is to lose the kind of (poetic) thinking most valued by the literary analyst. Even assuming that all thought occurs in language, this would suggest that the language of thought is not solely the language of univocal statement. Thus a sonnet can be highly rhetorical (containing a high density of conventional tropes) without simply trying to convince us of something: that beauty fades, that love is blind. And the loss incurred by paraphrasing a text is not a simply a loss of charm or decoration—or of persuasiveness, for that matter. Shakespeare's literary art is, to use a word popular in Shakespeare studies generally, a kind of perspectivism, allowing us to think about complex topics from multiple angles.[17] With Plato in mind, the notion of multiple perspectives is helpful for characterizing the contrapuntal movement—the simultaneous currents, countercurrents, and meandering trajectories of thought-in-language that we may recognize in and as literary discourse, and which are anathema to expository comprehension. And lest this aesthetic approach to the art of poetry seem to stray too far afield, let us not forget that Schleiermacher viewed Plato's misunderstood unification of form and content as the work of a "philosophical artist."[18] More recent scholars such as R. B. Rutherford, Charles Kahn, and Christopher Rowe have likewise made explicit gestures toward a philosophical aesthetic of sorts in seeking to account for Plato's literary "art" of philosophical writing.[19] And like Schleiermacher, scholars now wish to translate Plato's dialogue form so as to reveal its covert (by which I mean inapparent) purposefulness. This justifies but does not do justice to the dialogue form. As I see it, recent gestures toward the importance of artful writing tend to straitjacket the wayward play of language that is inherent and insistent in Plato's dialogue form, justifying that form as a persuasive tool Plato used to promote or impose a philosophical lesson or agenda.[20] Reassurances that literary form is not merely decorative thus end up saying that the literary is not only literary but also expository.

---

[17] Vendler herself does not use this term. For discussions of literary perspectivism, see Spitzer 1988, Burke 1969:503–517; cf. Cooper 1997:xxiii. Regarding perspectivism in Shakespeare, Russ McDonald notes that scholars have situated Shakespeare's own perspectivism among Early Modern conceptions of ancient rhetoric (2001:49). As a hermeneutic principle, perspectivism may be seen in the New Critical suggestion that literary criticism (unlike historical and philosophical interpretation) "is as much concerned with the processes of stylistic refraction as it is with the topics and ideas mediated by the literary text" (Bradford 1997:35).

[18] Schleiermacher 1936:4; Lamm 2000:222–226.

[19] Rutherford 1995; Kahn 1996; Rowe 2006, 2007.

[20] See e.g. Rowe 2007:12.

The Rhetorical Approach to Literary Form in Plato

Given the historical weight of literariness associated with Shakespeare, and with lyric poetry generally, the comparison with Plato may seem a poor one. As noted earlier, however, my argument does not, strictly speaking, rely on conventional categories of genre or discourse per se. These categories may seem to have been dictated by form—and most do have distinctive formal characteristics or qualities—but a category such as literary discourse is notoriously difficult to pin down in terms of formal features. To take a basic example, we may segregate verse (the arrangement of words in a rhythmic pattern) from poetry—an advertising jingle, for instance, is different from a text by Sappho—but this determination will always be a choice, made within limitations imposed by convention and context.[21] And a similar choice is involved in our treatment of rhetoric. Virtually any text we encounter will contain an array of identifiable rhetorical devices. When we wish to retrieve a uniform message (a teaching, let us say) from the text, then its rhetoric cannot be allowed to distract us from the goal of comprehension and conviction. On the contrary, rhetoric must somehow help turn us toward that goal, which is then shared by both reader and text; otherwise, rhetoric will be discounted or ignored. Should the text's language at times seem bent or deviant, the interpreter must straighten it out; justifying the means by the end, explaining away local turns as inevitable detours in a global plan, and reducing dialogical currents to a static, authoritative monologue.[22] Indeed, for the expository interpreter of rhetoric, figurative language is only apparently figurative; in the end, those elements of the text that are deemed figurative must be literalized, regularized, or discarded. It is in this way that allegorical interpretation is another kind of expository literalization, assigning a fixed and correct sense to each (figurative, yet manifest) element of the text in order to recover a single (literal, but latent) message.

In *Plato and the Art of Philosophical Writing* (2007), Christopher Rowe proposes to explain Plato's "strategies as a writer who writes, for the most part, in order to *persuade* his readers…. In other words, my first concern is with understanding the nature of Platonic *rhetoric*" (vii).[23] While Rowe's specific take on Plato is distinctive, the approach to rhetoric described in his book, an approach that is also forcefully laid out in his article "The Literary and Philosophical Style of the *Republic*" (2006), may serve to represent the view of literary form that

---

[21] See Hollander 2001:1–2.

[22] On the metalinguistics of metaphor as turning, see Nietzsche 2010; Culler 1975, 2002; Derrida 1984; Lakoff and Johnson 2003; Schur 1998.

[23] Quoting a definition of rhetoric from the OED, Rowe writes, "If rhetoric is 'the art of using language so as to persuade or influence others,' Plato has a fair claim to be the inventor, as well as the finest proponent, of *philosophical* rhetoric" (2007:268).

I am criticizing here.[24] Rowe's conception of persuasive rhetoric is shared by many scholarly attempts to understand Plato as a philosophical writer, and so I will now point out some of its salient characteristics. As I noted earlier, the nonexpository form of Plato's dialogues has become a major problem for philosophical interpretation. And one attractive way to frame the problem ("the longest-running dispute among Plato's interpreters") is in terms of Platonism: "what it is that Plato stands for" (Rowe 2007:2). On the one hand, Plato may have wanted readers to think for themselves, yet the abundance of arguments and positions in the dialogues points many toward dogmatism; and for Rowe, the sheer reiteration of a claim, along with the passion seen in its formulation, can argue strongly for Plato's commitment to it (2006:8–9). On the other hand, "if Plato is so anxious to communicate, or at any rate get us thinking about, certain substantive theses," asks Rowe, "why does he go about it in so roundabout a way?" (2006:9).[25] In response to this question, Rowe proceeds to invoke a conception of distance, to which I will return in my next chapter; in essence, "Plato's use of the dialogue form reflects his recognition of the distance that separates his own assumptions from those of any likely reader."[26] But my first concern is with the notion of persuasive rhetoric itself, which allows Rowe to explain Plato's digressive, "roundabout way" of writing in terms of purposefulness, arguing that Plato is using "strategies" to promote "substantive theses."

To begin with, Rowe, like most interpreters, assumes that Plato was a philosophical writer (2007:1). Similarly, most of us assume that Plato wrote these complex and thought-provoking texts in order to share and, crucially, to teach us something that he knew, whether this be the truth or the way to truth. Rowe acknowledges that the term *philosophy* can mean a variety of things (2007:9), but he, like most interpreters, consistently takes it as a coherent system of interconnected propositions held by an individual thinker, as in the phrase "what it is that Plato stands for." (Even those who attribute a less systematic, more searching stance to Plato tend to look for a coherent account of what Plato thought and what he wanted us to think. Anything less would be too vague

---

[24] Rowe poses his view of Plato and Socrates against, in particular, what he sees as skeptical developmentalism, on the one hand, and strict doctrinalism, on the other; he seeks to discern and explain Plato's varied but purposeful strategies of writing, which persuasively acclimate readers to a coherent set of ideas that may then serve as "starting-points" for further thought (2007:1–51; see also Penner and Rowe 2005:196–205). Rowe's emphasis on unity, connectedness, and purposefulness recalls Schleiermacher, in particular.

[25] Cf. a question rehearsed in Rowe 2007: "why on earth did Plato not try to impart his teaching in a more direct way?" (3).

[26] Plato's "aim is to draw *us* over from where are now to where *he* is; and to that end he employs a variety of persuasive devices" (Rowe 2006:10; cf. 2007:25, 31, 55.). Words such as "aim" and "end" reflect a teleological conception of "devices," identifiable, conventionally rhetorical structures that are used purposefully to achieve a univocal (expository) agenda.

to count as a philosopher's philosophy.) As the English word *stand* indicates, philosophy involves taking fixed positions. A position (a propositional claim) set forth by the philosopher is a thesis, and is substantive by virtue of the thinker's commitment to it. (As discussed in the next chapter, a literary *theme* is a topic but not a position.) According to Rowe, for instance, one of the positions obviously taken by Plato in the *Republic* is that justice pays (2006:9).[27] When it comes to philosophy, the author is presumed to be using the instrument of writing to endorse and promote certain theses. And this is what *univocal* means: declarative, assertive; argumentative; promoting a single, authorial point of view—all of which amounts to a definition of expository writing. To repeat Frye's definition, "philosophy is assertive or propositional writing" (1957:329). Given these assumptions, the idea that Plato is using language persuasively makes great sense. As a philosopher and teacher, how could he not be trying to make as strong a case as possible for his philosophy?

Nevertheless, this explanation does not solve so much as it finesses the long-standing problem of literary form, particularly as sharpened by Schleiermacher's insistence on the connectedness of form and content. Before returning to the example of Rowe, I would like to offer a clearer view of what is meant in this context by *literary form*. For interpreters of Plato the philosopher, literary form is not only a collection of features that we moderns (following in Plato's and Aristotle's footsteps) have conventionally deemed "literary" (fictionality, setting, characterization, and the like), although simply by being identifiable, these features are of great significance. Instead, literary form in Plato is defined negatively: it is any form of discourse that is not manifestly declarative. This version of the literary can be identified linguistically as a nondeclarative mode of discourse. Of course, the dialogues are replete with declarative sentences that make propositional statements, but apart from the letters, none of Plato's works, not even the *Apology*, is an example of global declaration. This is why, at the broadest level of description, we can speak of Plato's varied experimentations in *the dialogue form*, a genre of presentation marked first and foremost by the fact that Plato does not declare his commitment and does not speak in the first person. The dialogues are therefore, by definition, not univocal. By the same token, the literary face of Plato's discourse—defined as the obverse of authorial discourse, which is a sine qua non for philosophical interpretation—is perceived as inherently mediated, refracted, and refractory. The dialogues are considered indirect because we assume that Plato is trying to give us direction; they are considered digressive and disorienting insofar as we are looking for the sort of straightforward, purposeful positions that

---

[27] Cf. White 1979:13–30.

constitute a philosophy such as Platonism. (Again, no one routinely attributes univocal systems to writers *as writers of literature*. One can imagine an expository Homerism, Virgilism, Danteism, Keatsism, Rimbaudism, or Proustism, but the effort is either misguided or of use only for limited purposes far removed from written compositions.)

At the same time, very few interpreters deny that Plato's dialogues are roundabout or indirect in their presentation of ideas. In his essay on literary and philosophical style, Rowe writes about the tremendous complexity of the *Republic*, its "indirection, its tangled plot," and "the *apparent* informality of its style" (2006:9, my emphasis). Rowe faces the unruliness of the *Republic* head-on: "themes, arguments, *apparent* digressions appear in such rapid succession that it is easy for the reader to lose his or her way" (2006:7, my emphasis).[28] Characterization in the dialogue, for instance, cannot be "for merely ornamental purposes," because "it is so obtrusive" (2007:11). Rather than ignore such impediments to the flow of univocal argument, Rowe, like Schleiermacher, seeks to convince us that they are purposeful, the operative term here being "apparent."[29] For, again recalling Schleiermacher, Rowe's vision of unity requires making a strong separation between the appearance of a disconnected presentation and the reality of philosophical substance. And here we see again how attention to the significance of form may lead away from merely apparent unruliness to consistent content. Rowe is sympathetic to the idea that "underlying the play of each and every dialogue, there is a kind of subterranean flow of thought that is ... constant" (2006:8). All readers perceive the manifest, superficial play of language, but that play is merely apparent, underpinned as it supposedly is by a unified and single current of thought. Therefore, "underlying the whole grand edifice" of the *Republic* "is a substantive, and connected, set of ideas, which needs to be carefully excavated and reconstructed" (2006:9).[30] In his effort to find a global "set of ideas"—which is not different from the ideas we read about in Plato so much as a substantive (authorial, authoritative) and connected (coherent, quasisyllogistic) version of them—Rowe adopts a methodology that is compelled to look beyond or beneath what is actually there. Although this approach tries to avoid the cherry-picking of arguments so often found in traditional readings of Plato, it is a project of excavation and reconstruction, unable to rely on the evidence present to our senses—if anything, it

---

[28] Compare the references to digression (*abschweifen*, Tennemann 1792:127) and "disconnectedness" (*Unzusammenhang*, Schleiermacher 1836:8–9) quoted above.

[29] See Rowe 2007:2n2 for a related and explicit emphasis on the term "apparent." Compare Schleiermacher's "apparently" (1836:37–38), quoted above.

[30] Compare Schleiermacher's stress on "connectedness" (*Zusammenhang*, 1836:8).

encourages us to tamper with the evidence. (Like Schaerer, Rowe could be said to argue that what is actually written is merely a world of appearances.)

The notion of rhetorical persuasion has thus given scholars a way to explain the peculiarity of the dialogue form as Plato developed it. Again, the problem may be summed up roughly as follows: Why did Plato experiment with variations on the dialogue form rather than write in an expository manner? Once we recognize the power of philosophical rhetoric, a question concerning Plato's motives, aims, and goals itself becomes rhetorical, and we will be ready to accept literary form as a device or instrument in the service of philosophy; as a detour, that is, on our teleological journey to recover the philosopher's didactic agenda. So David Gallop asks, "How can literary form, by endowing philosophical argument with an appropriate 'rhetoric,' enable it to achieve its goals?" The popularity of the rhetorical approach can be glimpsed in the following subtitles of books: *The Philosophical Use of a Literary Form* (Kahn 1996), *Literary Device and Dramatic Structure in Plato's Dialogues* (Gordon 1999), *Rhetoric As Philosophy* (Michelini 2003), and *Plato's Many Devices* (Scott 2007). As Jill Gordon puts it, "what to modern eyes and ears are literary elements of Plato's texts ... are not embellishments, or finery, or even mere artistry. Rather, they are necessary for Plato to achieve his philosophical aim" (1999:12). If literary form is to be defended, in the name of philosophical writing and against charges of ornamentation and uselessness, Plato's art must be more artful and less arty, it seems. This is also the force (or rather the weakness) of the word *art* in studies by philosophers such as Rutherford, Kahn, and Rowe; scholars who celebrate Plato's artistry by pitting the writer's control and the writing's usefulness against Plato's apparent renunciation of authority and the apparent dilatoriness of the dialogue form. Thus the literary aspect of writing is converted into the expository art of rhetoric.[31]

In his book on the *Phaedrus*, G. R. F. Ferrari shares this attitude when he explains the function of the dialogue's physical setting: "This mode of exposition—Plato's device of orienting his readers by narrating how his characters orient themselves and their landscape—is no literary toy"; on the contrary, stresses Ferrari, it "has philosophic purpose" (1987:2). Ferrari's contextually sensitive analysis of topography in the dialogue is compelling, but here we see an attempt to justify literary form as an expository "device" that guides readers toward a philosophical end. By claiming that the setting of the *Phaedrus* is not a "literary toy" but a philosophical tool, Ferrari does two things at once—bucking traditional scholarship by arguing for the significance of literary form, yet also

---

[31] A related version of Platonic writing is seen in the notion of "logographic necessity," adopted from the *Phaedrus* as a hermeneutic principle. See Clay 2000:110–114; Strauss 1964:53.

seeking disciplinary legitimacy by implying that the literary is merely literary (and therefore a plaything) unless we can demonstrate its single-minded purposefulness. Such an attitude (made all the more complicated by the contrapuntal way rhetoric is toyed with in the *Phaedrus* itself) shows how expository treatments can dismiss the text's literariness as merely apparent.

Twentieth-Century Rhetorical Analysis

Meanwhile, it is a twentieth-century innovation to delve into the figurative dimension of manifestly and avowedly univocal prose, and the rhetorical analysis of literary form in Plato is likewise a radical and previously unexplored approach. It is an irony of intellectual history that the rhetorical approach to Plato echoes selected developments in literary studies, and discussion of these interdisciplinary similarities is usually avoided. In the analysis of Plato as a writer of textual artifacts, the modern emphasis on form has significant points of resemblance to literary formalism, in general, and to the New Criticism in particular. Many of the principles guiding the nondogmatic interpretation of Plato, such as "holism, contextualism, and organicism" (Press 1993b:111), are recognizably New Critical concepts. Blondell stresses that a text-based understanding of the dialogues must accept "the fundamental literary-critical axiom that every detail of the text contributes to the meaning of the whole."[32] Given the ongoing influence of the New Criticism in academic textual analysis generally, its incursion into the study of philosophy should come as no surprise, especially if scholars of Plato are indeed, as R. B. Rutherford puts it, now "using tools of literary analysis."[33] What makes things more unusual in the case of Plato is simply the potential dissonance between literary concepts of interpretation and philosophical conceptions of writing. Writers have produced works of genre-busting literary philosophy or philosophical literature throughout history (to name just a few: Parmenides, Lucretius, Boethius, Rousseau, Kierkegaard, Nietzsche, Sartre, and Blanchot), but the literary analysis of philosophical rhetoric is a methodological development that flourished in the last quarter of the twentieth century, with the advent of Deconstruction. The title of a book by

---

[32] Blondell 2002:4, with note 8. As Blondell also points out, this holistic organicism is a decidedly modern hermeneutic principle, but it may be well suited to interpreting Plato's ancient texts, depending on the reader's agenda (2002:5).

[33] Rutherford writes that he and his colleagues have been "using tools of literary analysis to shed light on Plato's method of working, which is ... very far from that of a modern writer of philosophic textbooks" (2002:250).

Christopher Norris, *The Deconstructive Turn: Essays in the Rhetoric of Philosophy* (1983), sums up several aspects of the movement.[34]

Although more recent rhetorical approaches to Plato share with Deconstruction an interest in the literary form of philosophy and in the analysis of rhetoric, scholars of Plato have maintained a traditional view of rhetoric as a technical means of persuasion, choosing not to follow literary studies in this regard. In this instance, a specific interdisciplinary gap between philosophical and literary studies mirrors the general difference between expository and literary methods of interpretation. In the twentieth century, scholars of literature began developing a new conception of rhetoric, focused on the plurisignificant potential of figurative language, that was more suited to their concerns than was the traditional notion of rhetoric as persuasion. Thomas Cole suggests that this "neorhetoric" (whether formalist, structuralist, or deconstructionist) bears so little resemblance to the old discipline as to be a symptom of our "antirhetorical" times (1991:20).[35] Whereas ancient rhetoric assumes a "separability of matter from method," this principle "is incompatible with the central position that close reading and interpretation of texts has come to occupy in literary studies" (19). Furthermore, ancient rhetoric "undergoes what is in effect a complete inversion when ... its contents are now studied with an eye on the multiplication rather than—as in antiquity—the reduction of meaning in any given piece of artistic discourse" (21). Cole's observations help to show how the neorhetorical tools of twentieth-century literary criticism (wherewith one strives to maintain the inseparability of thought and language throughout the interpretation of a written composition) are incompatible with the traditional, expository conception of rhetoric currently being applied to Plato.

The modern conception of rhetoric is descriptive. Harking back to Nietzsche and Freud, it is part of the linguistic turn that occurred in the humanities during the twentieth century, especially in its literary-theoretical recognition that language is rarely, if ever, transparent or neutral. Besides the art of persuasion, which is a prescriptive arsenal of techniques developed in conjunction with ancient oratory and adapted to the purposes of writing, rhetoric has also become a descriptive resource for textual analysis.[36] Influential and self-consciously innovative conceptions of rhetoric were brought to the study of

---

[34] Norris's title contains echoes of the "linguistic turn" (Rorty), Heidegger's "turning," and the turns of metaphor as trope. Derrida 1983 ("Plato's Pharmacy") is the seminal text in this regard.

[35] See Kenneth Burke, "Rhetoric—Old and New" (1967). Bradford 1997: "Rhetoric has been variously transformed into modern stylistics. The New Critics and the Formalists are the most obvious inheritors of the disciplines of rhetoric" (13).

[36] "Rehabilitators of rhetoric in the twentieth century have set themselves two goals: to achieve a total rhetoric, and to make it descriptive rather than prescriptive. A total rhetoric would address all aspects of textual construction, global as well as local" (Chatman 1990:185).

literature by I. A. Richards (*The Philosophy of Rhetoric*, published in 1936), Kenneth Burke (*A Grammar of Motives*, 1945), and Wayne Booth (*The Rhetoric of Fiction*, 1961). And new types of rhetorical analysis, inflected by Russian formalism, structural linguistics, and semiotics (especially through the influence of Roman Jakobson) were also developed by Roland Barthes, Jacques Derrida, and Paul de Man. Meanwhile, major strands of literary stylistics and narratology evolved as literary-rhetorical counterparts of linguistic specialties such as discourse analysis, pragmatics, and text linguistics. I offer merely a few indications of these academic trends in order to situate this aspect of my argument in a critical tradition.

In *The Philosophy of Rhetoric*, Richards chooses to focus on "how words work in discourse" (1965:5). "My subject," writes Booth, "is the technique of non-didactic fiction, viewed as the art of communicating with readers—the rhetorical resources available to the writer of epic, novel, or short story as he tries, consciously or unconsciously, to impose his fictional world upon the reader" (1983:xiii). Barthes's explicit reassessment of rhetoric may be found in essays such as "Rhetorical Analysis" (1966), "From Science to Literature" (1967), and "Style and Its Image" (1969), collected in the *The Rustle of Language* (1986). In "Semiology and Rhetoric," de Man chooses to understand rhetoric as "the study of tropes and figures" rather than what he calls "the derived sense of comment or of eloquence or persuasion" (1973:28). Concurrent with the trend toward rhetorical description came an emphasis on overdetermination, insofar as factors beyond the author's avowed or implied sense of purpose have been increasingly thought to contribute significantly to the structuring, wording, and functioning of texts.[37] As a descriptive approach focused on the functioning of discourse, rhetorical analysis offers an expanded vocabulary (adapted mainly from ancient rhetoric) for identifying patterns or structures of language, and for connecting these structures with significant functions and effects. Neorhetoric can allow for many different and concurrent functions.

As it is, literary works, unlike expository ones, are routinely presumed to communicate more than just fixed positions (lessons, morals, and the like); at the same time, many interpreters of literature share a "common view that literary texts can be interpreted equally well in vastly different and deeply incompatible ways."[38] It is in this sense that literary works are said to be overdetermined (without, it must be stressed, being open to every possible interpretation).[39] The

---

[37] See Cole 1991:21–22.

[38] Nehamas 1985:3.

[39] Rowe exhibits a particularly offhand disregard for the overdetermination of texts (2006:9–10). Rowe raises the specter of "varieties of relativism in literary theory," wielding the term *relativism*—itself a fashionable and politically charged bogey—to dismiss the possibility that the

term *overdetermination*, coined by Freud, refers to the way multiple factors or causes can contribute to a single manifestation (such as a detail in a dream or a symptom in an illness of complex origins).[40] Thus in literary studies, a word may be considered overdetermined insofar as it is recognized to have a plurality of meanings at the same time. The term is especially apt for describing polysemy, when expository interpretation must suppress potential contradictions in order to maintain a stable, univocal meaning. If one allows that no text is exclusively, single-mindedly purposeful, then interesting patterns of form and relevant currents of nonargumentative significance may be rewardingly observed in expository texts—*and* in the Platonic dialogues, especially since the latter have never been thought to fit into a neat opposition between literary and nonliterary. Regardless of broad formal conventions that might tell us when language is literary or philosophical, the language in a dialogue can have other notable functions besides communicating expository content and promoting authorial positions.

Thus the modern conception of rhetoric also shifts attention toward text-oriented functions (how does the text work and what is it doing?) at the expense of didacticism and straightforward direction (what is the text teaching us and what is it telling us to do?). Such an emphasis on multiple functions recognizes that all texts communicate ideological implications, without concluding that this is all they do and that they do this univocally. Textualism of this sort is relatively familiar to interpreters of literature, but it is rather alien to classicists steeped in historical reconstruction, and it has little purchase among philosophers who wish to recover what a historical individual actually thought.[41]

Still, none of this is particularly radical; scholars in many disciplines now have an ingrained awareness that conventional categories of discourse are entangled: "avowedly literary" texts contain all sorts of mundane or nonliterary utterances, while "all texts have secret-hidden-deeper meanings, and none more so than the supposedly obvious and straightforward productions of journalists, historians, and philosophers."[42] In fact, a growing awareness of this dimension of rhetoric accompanied the contemporary resurgence of philosophical interest in the literary form of Plato's texts in the 1980s. Introducing *Platonic*

Republic might convey multiple and contradictory currents of thought, rather than standing as a single ideological edifice (which must nevertheless be "excavated and reconstructed"). See also Annas 2000:34.

[40] Freud 1953:283–284.

[41] For a defense of historically oriented intentionalism, see Heath 2002. For a wide-ranging argument against giving special consideration to authorial intention over other kinds of evidence, see Maynard 2009, who suggests that, their usefulness notwithstanding, "historical interpretations are only other interpretations" (30).

[42] Scholes 1985:8.

Writings/Platonic Readings in 1988, Charles L. Griswold, Jr. called this period "the era of 'deconstruction'" (2002:15). Suggesting that the analysis of many canonical philosophical texts could benefit from attention to their "*literary* integrity," Griswold contemplated the possibility that "the rhetorical devices frequently deprecated by philosophers ... are inseparable from even the most systematic or architectonic works. How authoritative or final is the apparent divorce of philosophy from rhetoric and poetics?" (15). Despite the great progress that has been made in pursuing these questions and in raising the profile of literary features in the dialogues, avowedly literary approaches to Plato have remained focused largely on the didactic function of literary form. The need for fuller consideration of nonexpository functions of literary form in Plato remains, and my next chapter will suggest that Plato's manifest repudiation of authority is, among other things, just that: a rhetoric of qualification.

Schleiermacher's Legacy

Because the dogmatic approach distorts the compositional integrity of the writings, a conundrum arises when one seeks both to avoid constructing a dogmatic Plato and at the same time to reconstruct and extract Plato's thought, as though it were merely distorted but still essentially encrypted in those same writings. Plato's writing would thus remain a tool that could be *used* to reach a predefined pedagogical end. By treating literary form as persuasive rhetoric, interpreters make an end run around the overt unruliness of Plato's writing and arrive back at rather fixed, regularized conclusions. This utilitarian conception refuses to accept the dialogical implications of dialogical form. It subsumes literary form under expository philosophy by placing Plato's text in the rhetorical service of his presumed purpose: namely, to advance his didactic agenda and univocal teachings, whether these be gently propaedeutic, maieutic, protreptic, or coercive.

To summarize, I see the rhetorical explanation of Plato's literary form that stems from Schleiermacher's holism as a misguided development, on four grounds. First, its teleology is tautological; though not in itself wrong, it is unhelpful. Let us all agree that Plato, like any skilled writer in any literary or expository genre, strives to use language as effectively as possible. Beyond that, our understanding of literary form must look beyond traditional rhetoric for a satisfactory solution to the problem this form has come to present. And if we are not sure of Plato's goals, then we must be careful about allowing them to dictate our interpretive approach.

Second, an expository reading of Plato's dialogues does not respect their manifest form, but instead strives to subsume or convert that form into a desired, presumed content. (In the metaphorical topography of Schleiermacher and Rowe, the lack of univocal directedness in Plato's dialogues is declared superficial, though apt to lead the reader away from subterranean substances.[43]) In other words, I suggest that to read Plato's dialogues as *covertly expository*—as communicating fixed, yet unavowed messages installed in the text by the author and retrievable by the reader—is to read against the acknowledged grain of the texts, precisely by invalidating or recasting their obvious texture.

Third, to move from the unruly form of Plato's dialogues to the declarative, expository form of philosophical didacticism requires interpreters to perform an act of translation that is profoundly reductive, and self-contradictory in the way it argues that a manifestly open form is really, in the end, covertly closed.[44] And fourth, when literary form is assigned a philosophical, expository function, it is no longer literary (literary, I mean, in the sense that led the interpreter to call it literary in the first place).[45]

Each of these criticisms articulates the difference between expository and literary interpretation, a difference that does not hinge on the status of the text per se. Rhetorical persuasion is, to be sure, an inherently expository conception of function, and is therefore incompatible with a nonexpository, literary conception of form. Yet rather than bring new problems to the fore, the points I raise are reformulations of the problem first encountered by Plato's earliest readers, and then brought into relief by the likes of Schleiermacher and Schaerer. Few contemporary scholars of Plato claim to be literary interpreters, but many seek to account for the literary form of Plato's writings—if only by insisting that this so-called literary form is not, in essence, *merely* literary (or merely decorative) because it is also philosophical. Some would prefer to erase the traditional division between philosophy and literature entirely, but here too the tendency is to show that the literary can have a philosophical function that mere literature does not.

Striving to save Plato's literary form for the purposes of Platonism, some scholars seek to identify devices, strategies, and uses that could align the text

---

[43] Cf. Kahn 1996: "*behind* the literary *fluctuations* of Plato's work *stands* the *stable* world view defined by his commitment to an otherworldly metaphysics" (xv–xvi, my emphasis).

[44] Rowe 2006: "The approach I shall adopt in this chapter is to reject absolutely the possibility that Plato intended to leave his readers with an open text, that is, a text on which the reader is free to place his or her own interpretation" (8–9). Rowe must rely on a self-confirming intentionalist premise (prioritizing what he is certain that Plato intended) in order to argue for an expository model of authorial message-making as opposed to a literary model of mediation, pluralism, perspectivized ideas, linguistic patterning, and overdetermination.

[45] As Todorov 2007:27 says of literature: "Unlike religious, moral or political discourse, it does not formulate a system of precepts." See Culler 2007:233, who notes that de Man's version of rhetorical analysis fought against critics' use of literature to broadcast precepts.

with classical rhetoric, which assigns to all formal features the single overarching function of persuasion. But this approach relies on a single vision of philosophy that has never easily squared with Plato's idiosyncratic writings. If we adopt a modern and descriptive view of Plato's texts—not trying to reconstruct what ancient readers must have experienced, but staying within the realm of what Plato's Greek *could* have signified in his time—there can be no single answer concerning the function of literary form, but some features are more prominent and some functions more important than others. My approach in what follows is to expand and expound on prevalent patterns of self-reflection in the dialogues that are undervalued by interpreters of Plato's writings. When Plato's texts and his speakers reflect on their own methods, especially when they talk about talking, they often pose questions about the practice of philosophy that we have learned to ignore.

3

Literary Practice, Modality, and Distance

T HE PREVIOUS TWO CHAPTERS discussed hermeneutic problems and rarely touched on solutions. Positive goals conventionally associated with literary-rhetorical methods of reading were mentioned, but they remain to be explained more fully in the context of interpreting Plato's dialogues. As I will continue to argue, a powerful teleological impulse directs readers to seek single-minded and persuasive arguments in works that are, nonetheless, manifestly not univocal. The drive to explain literary form is one of the main factors that compel readers to reconstruct a covert univocality from Plato's dialogues. This chapter begins with some positive methodological suggestions that are eventually directed toward Plato's *Republic*. After reviewing some hermeneutic concepts that distinguish the modern rhetorical analysis of tropes—concepts such as relative emphasis, overdetermination, and modality—I introduce some specific tropes of distancing that emphasize and express remoteness throughout the *Republic*. Literary interpretation generally treats texts as highly mediated forms of communication, allowing that authors are more or less remote from what their texts say. And this same kind of remoteness is, I argue, given considerable weight in the *Republic*, both as a linguistic phenomenon and as a methodological topic.

The general problem of the dialogue form's digressive and indirect presentation of ideas is compounded by perplexing "ambiguities, obscurities, gaps, and contradictions" that pervade the characters' arguments.[1] These are so prevalent in the dialogues, observes E. N. Tigerstedt, that Plato may seem to have introduced them intentionally, as though his aim were not to satisfy "our legitimate claim for clarity and coherence but rather to derive a malicious pleasure from eluding it."[2] This is a strange thought, worth considering further: while making tantalizing gestures toward clarity and coherence, Plato may actually

---

[1] Tigerstedt 1977:15, cf. 24, 92.

[2] Tigerstedt, in a chapter called "The Problem," is here paraphrasing Heinrich von Stein's description of the hapless, uninitiated reader's plight on encountering Plato's dialogues (1977:15); the problem is the interpretation of Plato in the face of how Plato wrote his dialogues.

be *methodically elusive*. The strangeness can be erased by insisting that Plato's elusiveness is always and only an apparent deviation from methodical communication—but genuinely methodical elusiveness is a surprising phenomenon. Although Plato's writings are usually readily comprehensible, says Tigerstedt, "it is often difficult to be sure of what he really means" (14). I understand this basic difficulty in the interpretation of Plato as a constant struggle against the waywardness, the unpredictable and unexpected deviance, of his written texts. In other words, each elusive dialogue is pointing in multiple different and at times irreconcilable directions, while the interpreter typically seeks to find a path that leads from Plato the author to a univocal, promotional message—a philosophy of some sort—that supposedly must have inhered in the text from the start. Yet to carve such a straight path out of Plato's elusiveness is to disregard integral aspects of the text.

If we are to avoid assuming that the dialogues are covertly univocal tracts—which is entirely different from assuming, as I do, that each text is a fixed communication composed in words by a single author—then it will be best to treat each dialogue as a separate text. In the current chapter, I look to Plato's *Republic* in an effort to account for one dialogue's literary features, without trying to circumvent them or otherwise explain them away. I choose to focus on the *Republic* for several reasons: its current popularity and influence make it an exemplary object of study, its length allows broad patterns as well as details to emerge as demonstrably significant, and its self-conscious procedural discourse (seen in characters' frequent references to their own conversation) highlights waywardness as a thematic concern. This self-consciousness, or reflexivity, is itself a salient example of the now modern-seeming literariness that was already present in Plato's writing.

A Literary Practice of Interpretation

If we are to address the literary form of the *Republic*, and if we are to do so in a manner that accepts the work's literariness, then a fuller account of some literary-rhetorical working principles is needed, regardless of how different each individual interpreter's practice will be. While scholars working on literary form in Plato have been faulted for having less success with interpretive close readings than with metaphilosophical speculation, here I have been raising concerns about a more basic and metatextual stumbling block: namely, a fundamental difference between expository and literary conceptions of how texts function.[3] (Guilty of dwelling extensively on a metatextual question, I myself can only protest that the question has blocked my way and consumed my interest as a reader of Plato's text.)

Those on one side of this methodological divide maintain a traditional view of rhetoric, where many factors (including the historicizing goals long associated with philology and philosophy) foster a linear, teleological focus on literary elements as building blocks of argumentation and rhetorical persuasion. This, I have contended, is a serious hermeneutic limitation with regard to literary form. Modern rhetorical analysis, on the other side, brings with it a degree of freedom in this respect, by not requiring interpreters to derive a single persuasive agenda (a programmatic ideology or moral) from a writer's verbal maneuvers. Simply put, for a literary interpretation broadly conceived, all texts have many functions; perform many acts, both pragmatic and aesthetic; and advance many ideologies simultaneously.[4] Which raises a consequential concern: how are we to make discerning choices? Such a question can hardly receive a full treatment here. For clarifying my approach to the *Republic*, however, the modern interpretation of verbal rhetoric is perhaps best understood as a matter of emphasis. The following rationale for describing and interpreting language owes much to linguistics, but it goes far beyond that discipline's boundaries. Instead, it undergirds a method of humanistic cultural self-understanding.[5]

For the sake of clarity, the kind of modern and literary rhetorical analysis I have in mind can be defined as the description of tropes and the interpretation of their functions. As in ancient rhetoric, the tropes described by modern rhetorical analysis are identifiable uses of language that deviate (turn away) from standards of literal, prosaic expression. They exceed and enrich the norm of literal, denotative expression. But if the effects created by the tactics of ancient oratory are measured by the extent to which they support a speaker's ultimate, single-minded, pragmatic strategy of persuasion, the modern interpretation of tropes allows for their participation in multiple, simultaneous patterns of written language, so that currents and countercurrents of thought emerge through themes-as-expressed-in-language.

---

[3] For the suggestion that theories have fared better than interpretations in the study of Plato's literary form, see e.g. Cohn 2001:485, Rutherford 1995:26, Irwin 2002:199.

[4] In moving from sentence to discourse, linguistic description encounters a similar proliferation of functions in English, since even basic "clause types" (declarative, interrogative, exclamative, and imperative) are used in many ways, while combinations of sentences in discourse can be interpreted as speech acts having many direct and indirect pragmatic functions (illocutionary meanings). See CGEL 36, 61–62.

[5] Contrast the different project described by Irwin 2002, in which science may arrive at "true and historically accurate accounts of Plato" (199). See also Jeffries and McIntyre 2010:22–24 on objectivity in stylistics.

In practice, two basic policies may serve, when combined, as a schematic antidote to expository approaches that limit Plato's rhetoric to a univocal purpose. First, a literary hermeneutic will recognize patterns essentially by allocating attention and interest, which can be quite different from trying to trace a linear argument through a text. Formal-semantic patterns are construed in different ways by different readers, but each reading or interpretation is anchored in specific textual evidence. Careful analysis of a text requires attending to the interplay of language occasioned by specific wording. In terms devised by Roman Jakobson and associated with Russian formalism, wording consists of the text's syntagmatic arrangement and its paradigmatic selection of diction, which are interrelated in complex patterns.[6] When observing and describing these patterns—accounting for local details and global structures in complex systems of wording—readers allocate more attention to some details and less to others, depending on their perception of emphasis in the text. For this reason, guided by emphasis and interest, reading becomes a dynamic balance of attention and inattention, rather than a search for hidden meanings and covert authorial agendas. This aspect of critical practice is well served by the formalist principle of foregrounding, which identifies significance by noting textural patterns of similarity (parallelism, repetition) and contrast (deviation).[7]

The second policy, which concerns polysemy, provides an inseparable semantic complement to the formalist description of emphasis and patterning. Rather than suppress plurisignification for the sake of univocality, an operative literary approach to texture will give ample consideration to multiple, concurrent meanings when deciding what is important. In the examination of details and when drawing together broad thematic trends, emphasis (and therefore significance) attaches to elements that exhibit redundancy, overlap, and semantic plenitude. Here we have the principle of overdetermination, which accords greater relative significance to elements that participate in multiple patterns of meaning simultaneously. Closely related to overdetermination is the idea of mutual reinforcement.[8] Constituents of all types may share mutual connections, each exerting more or less gravity, so to speak, depending on whether it is more or less polyvalent and on its proximity to others. Each one can gain weight from multiple directions and thereby become an increasingly relevant part of the patterns to which it belongs. To indulge in a metaphor of

---

[6] See Jakobson, "Linguistics and Poetics" (1987:62–94); Lyons 1968:70–81.

[7] Jeffries and McIntyre 2010:30–34; Hawkes 2003:44–99; Fowler 1996:92–109; see Adams 1992 for Shklovsky, Mukarovsky.

[8] Cf. the approach to language generally in CGEL: "The full support for a decision in grammatical description consists of confirmation from hundreds of mutually supportive pieces of evidence" (2002:21).

my own: a polyvalent detail with a dance card full of other, related elements is a more meaningful one; a well-attended dance is a more inviting one; and each text is hosting multiple dances.

Within the parameters just described, literary emphasis—not bound to the reconstruction of an ultimate, single argument—is always construed as relative; and it is mainly in this sense that interpretation may become holistic and contextual.[9] Furthermore, literary interpretation is obliged to be pluralistic: differentiations in texture display concurrent patterns of emphasis, and no text is an undifferentiated block of argument. In academic practice, it is de rigueur to present one's literary reading as though it were the correct one; in practice, though, success is achieved by explaining how the evidence functions in interesting, important, significant ways.[10] Interpreters of Plato's writing who do not acknowledge the value of relative emphasis in form, and the validity of pluralism in meaning, will continue to convert the dialogues into expository treatises.[11]

If not quite the enemy, overdetermination is at least the antithesis of univocality in rational argument and in figurative representation. The linear focus needed to pursue logical argument through the variables introduced by literary form must be narrow, and must remain insensitive to the potential for words to interact in unexpected and unpredictable ways. What Helen Vendler calls the "unifying play of mind and language" is inevitably the variable interplay between words, their meanings, and the constellations that emerge into the foreground between text and reader (1997:5). Similarly, as long as each element, combination, and text (like a word, a phrase, and a sentence) participates in different constellations, then forceful attempts to regularize the text's combinatorial universe will result in nearsighted underinterpretation. Thus underinterpretation puts just as much of a strain on Plato's language as does overinterpretation. And allegorizing treatments of figurative expression, by assigning a fixed group of meanings to a fixed grouping of figures, ultimately transform the figurative potential of manifestly nonliteral features into covert, univocal, and literal messages.

Even from this abstract overview, it should be fairly clear that I am describing literary practice as a dynamic process. While navigating through strikingly different types of evidence, one's view of some evidence changes in

---

[9]   Cf. Hirsch 1976, esp. 41–44 on "patterns of emphasis" and "relative emphasis."

[10]   See Heath 2002:39–57. A simple example: Hirsch, even when arguing that we must judge between two incompatible interpretations of a poem (Brooks versus Bateson on Wordsworth), nevertheless gives the impression that both readings are quite successful (1976:41–51). Certainly, neither is deemed a failure.

[11]   E.g. Crombie on the "unifying theme—of which indeed Plato gives no plain statement" in the *Republic* (1962:74; see also 80). See below on possible differences, not observed in Crombie's terminology, between theme, thesis, and thematic statement.

view of other evidence. But it may not yet be clear where such an interpretation might lead, given my criticisms of the telos that guides expository approaches to the literary Plato. The task here is at any one time to reach a perspective on a theme as articulated in language by Plato, as opposed to a thesis that Plato supposedly held but left undeclared. In this regard, it is crucial to define some terms associated with *theme*. I take *theme* itself to denote an abstract topic that permeates a text, whether explicitly or implicitly. A theme is a topic of interest, a preoccupation that can emerge in different contexts and in different forms throughout a work—and which need not be addressed by the text in direct, linear discussion. So justice is a prominent theme in the *Republic*. A *thesis* is a proposition asserted as true by an author; this is the sort of claim typically advanced in expository writing. One thesis of my book is that the rhetorical patterning of Plato's *Republic* expresses, among many other things, a critical or questioning perspective on the conventional methods of investigation pursued by Socrates and his interlocutors.

A thematic *statement*, in contrast with a thesis, communicates a proposition that is not *asserted* by the author.[12] Such statements are propositions made in the text but not endorsed by the author. A statement about an important theme will naturally attract special attention. (This sort of unasserted statement is common in traditional forms of literature, being made by characters and narrators.) When, in Plato's *Republic*, the character Socrates is quoted (by Socrates the narrator) as saying "virtue has one form [*eidos*], but evil has countless forms" (ἓν μὲν εἶναι εἶδος τῆς ἀρετῆς, ἄπειρα δὲ τῆς κακίας, 445c), we have a thematic statement; one among countless others that may be found in the text.[13] In order to treat this as a thesis being asserted by Plato, interpreters must perform extra acts of literalization to establish Socrates as an allegorical equivalent of Plato— even when this equivalence will not consistently support the interpreter's reconstruction of the argument. On the one hand, Socrates, according to this procedure, is not really Socrates; on the other hand, what Socrates says as a figure is what Plato is really saying. According to the metaphorical metalanguage of literary criticism, this is an attempt to straighten out or regularize the twists of figurative language. Taking a literary speaker's thematic statement for an authorial thesis is typically considered a mistake in the literary practice of interpretation, but too much handwringing over this sort of intentional fallacy could obscure the prior necessity of making a decision between literary and nonliterary approaches.

---

12 See Lamarque and Olsen 1994:287, 321–338; along with Beardsley 1981:404.
13 Bloom's translation of the *Republic* (1968), frequently modified, has been used throughout because of its literal accuracy. The Greek edition used is that of Burnet (1903). Transliterated Greek words cited throughout the text may be found in the glossary.

Modality and the Qualification of Discourse

Born into a world shaped by Platonism, most readers of Plato will find it hard even to entertain the possibility that he may not have written simply and solely to persuade readers to adopt his own practices or beliefs. Despite the popular reverence for Socrates' professions of ignorance, he is generally viewed as a know-it-all, a character in the dialogues whose wisdom is exceeded only by that of his author Plato. Thus, as already described, we take Platonism to be a body of beliefs, constituting a philosophy that itself largely makes up philosophy as we know it. Equally relevant is the fact that many readers regularly and habitually aim to extract a moral (a main thesis or proposition endorsed and promoted by the author) not just from expository texts but also from decidedly literary ones as well. Scholars struggle over the moral of *Antigone* or *Hamlet* no less than they fret over the message of the *Republic*.[14] Effectively blinkered, readers may resolutely pursue such expository and literalistic goals, gathering and assessing information while shutting off multiple avenues of ongoing exploration. I am not arguing that readers cannot or should not read this way. I have, however, sought to explain why such a thesis-seeking approach must remain blind to the kind of textural complexity that is valued in the modern practice of literary criticism.

Intertwined with the conviction that Plato is trying to teach us lessons in a rhetorically persuasive manner is the assumption that he is endorsing and promoting the propositions (theses, points, and claims) expressed by his characters, especially the ideas introduced and advocated by his protagonist Socrates.[15] When an argument is brought to some kind of conclusion during a dialogue, this conclusion is viewed as a goal reached by Plato's composition. As a matter of course, many commentators do not hesitate to use tags such as "Plato thinks," "Plato believes," and "Plato says" to ascribe authorial arguments and assertions to the dialogues. Yet when Nicholas White, for instance, declares that "the aim of the *Republic* is very simple" (1979:13), he also recognizes substantial complications concerning the interpretation of "Plato's intentions" (12), pausing at one point during his summary of the dialogue's argument to observe that "another complication is the fact that the gap between Plato's actual view and what is generally attributed to him is even greater than what I have just said would lead one to suspect" (45).[16] White's commentary is a sensible

---

14 Cf. Heath 2002:11–16.
15 For extended discussions of Socrates as mouthpiece for Plato, see Corlett 2005; Cohn 2001; Press 2000; Wolfsdorf 1999; Edelstein 1998; Mulhern 1971.
16 According to White, the aim of the *Republic* is "to discover what justice (*dikaiosunē*) is, and to show that it is more beneficial, in a certain sense of that word, than its contrary, injustice (*adikia*)" (1979:13). Emlyn-Jones and Preddy: "Ostensibly the construction of a 'Kallipolis' ('beautiful,'

and practical contribution to the study of Platonism. I am simply noting that such gaps—between Plato's individually held views, the views expressed in his dialogues, and the views attributed to him by his interpreters—reflect profound complications.[17] As I have been suggesting, contemporary attempts to unify and neutralize Plato's dialogues under Plato's univocal control are not consonant with the composition of Plato's texts.

That said, the question of attribution is arguably less important than is the degree of Plato's commitment to the propositions expressed by his characters. Plato wrote many things, which is to say that he authored many statements. Yet his commitment to these utterances, I will argue, is consistently and globally characterized by ongoing circumspection. When dealing with propositions, philosophers and linguists often focus on a statement's truth value—whether the proposition expressed by a statement is true or false. And this is similar to the way professional philosophers are apt to judge arguments from Plato's dialogues, as if abducting these arguments from textual slumber in order to interrogate their independent integrity according to absolutist standards of logical reasoning. But while propositions themselves may be judged true or false, the way a proposition is specifically formulated in language is also an expression of the speaker's attitude. Through language, that is, "speakers commit themselves, to a greater or lesser degree, to what they are saying" (Matthews 1997, s.v. "assertive"). In linguistic terms, this degree of commitment, which contributes on a larger scale to our sense of the speaker's or author's cumulative stance and of the text's overall status, is signaled by grammatical forms and constructions that are categorized under the heading of *modality*.

Although modality continues to be debated by linguists and further complicated by developments in modal logic, a nontechnical version of the concept should be perfectly adequate for our purposes. When dealing with sentences, which is what most linguists do by trade, modality may be considered a semantic notion that comprises "the speaker's opinion or attitude towards the proposition that the sentence expresses or the situation that the proposition describes."[18] Just as most languages have a distinct and seemingly neutral or unmarked procedure for making declarative statements that the speaker "believes to be true" (Palmer 1986:26), modality usually refers to a hierarchical range of attitudes that diverge from the directness of certainty about facts

---

or 'fine city'), the purpose and aims of *Republic* are nevertheless far from straightforwardly expressed" (2013:1.ix). Cf. Reeve 1988:41–42; Crombie 1962:73–74.

[17] Complaints like that made by Burnyeat, who says that for Leo Strauss the *Republic* "means the opposite of what it says" (1999:300–301), ignore the difference between the conversation, in which characters say things, and the book, which does not state or assert anything.

[18] Lyons 1977:452; see Palmer 1986:1–23.

and reality.[19] The full range of modality or modalities is extraordinarily wide, covering territory from "possibility, probability, and necessity" to "permission, obligation, and requirement" (Palmer 1986:19). In general, though, modality is "the linguistic phenomenon whereby grammar allows one to say things about, or on the basis of, situations which need not be real" (Portner 2009:1). Among the many facets of modality, I wish to single out uses of language that address "situations which need not be real." In this general sense of modality, which I will be using henceforth, to *modalize* a statement (or a stretch of discourse) is to qualify it as more or less remote from certainty (or alternatively, possible or probable to some greater or lesser degree).

Although they have other important functions, the subjunctive and optative *moods* of the verb in ancient Greek are commonly used to signal that something may or might be the case. These moods are marked morphologically in verb forms, but semantic modality can also be expressed lexically, by specific verbs, adjectives, adverbs, and particles; and its presence can be determined by contextual cues, which takes us beyond semantics proper into the domain of pragmatics.[20] Linguistics has traditionally limited the scope of modality to the study of sentences, and to grammatical forms in particular, yet "many of the features associated with modality may not be marked grammatically" (Palmer 1986:5), and this is certainly the case in ancient Greek. Linguists have taken an interest in discourse modality and in the related phenomenon of hedging, but the idea of modalizing tropes remains an open area for research.[21] Of course, grammatical moods in Greek have a variety of conventional, as opposed to strictly logical or argumentative, functions. Politeness is a primary one. My point, however, is not that Socrates frequently hedges in the *Republic* (although he does); instead, such hedging gains in prevalence by being part of an even broader pattern in the text. Thus even when Socrates is simply being polite, Plato's composition—which operates far from the naïve simplicity of casual conversation—exhibits this politeness in a more self-aware and less socially conventional manner. Here I am proposing that modality offers a useful way to understand a major function of literary form in Plato's *Republic*.

As already discussed, defining literary discourse per se is impracticable, so that the operative issue is whether a stretch of discourse is construed as

[19] For considerations of the indicative as "unmodalized," see Lyons 1968:307–308; Palmer 1986:26–29; Duhoux 2000:179; CGEL 173.

[20] As Huddleston and Pullum put it, "mood is a category of grammar, modality a category of meaning. Mood is a grammaticalisation of modality within the verbal system" (CGEL 172; see also 33–43, 172–177). For a concise statement of reservations concerning such an account of mood, see Salkie 1988. On the modalities of the Greek verb, see Duhoux 2000:176–186.

[21] On discourse modality in linguistics, see Palmer 1986:91–94; Portner 2009:3–8. See Enkvist 1985 for a discussion exploring the place of rhetoric in stylistics.

literary by the interpreter. Lamarque and Olsen, whose definition of thematic statement I have adopted, stress the special lack of assertion (authorial endorsement or commitment) found in literary discourse. "A literary work," they write, "does indeed have themes or meanings which can be stated as propositions, but ... these propositions have a unique role in literary appreciation, which is not reducible to the role they might have in philosophy, religious discourse, or the social sciences" (1994:323).[22] The special status of these propositions in literary discourse is that they are nonasserted; or, in the terminology I am using, they are modalized. I should stress that statements of this sort are not empty gestures; thematic statements within recognized literary contexts "can be assigned significance and thus be understood without being construed as asserted" (328). As the discussions and arguments shared in Plato's writings should make clear, such tentative exploration need not be a superficial dip into shallow ideas. This is why I will not shy away from suggesting that literary form in the *Republic* allows for a positive and substantial depiction of methods that are nevertheless inconclusive in principle as well as practice.

Several scholars have described Plato's elusive stance in terms of distance, but their accounts have tended to fit it into their own pedagogical agendas, suggesting that Plato (covertly) uses the distance between himself and his audience to rhetorically persuasive effect.[23] The modalizing distance that I discern in the text of the *Republic* is more akin to the narratological category of distance described by Genette under the heading of narrative "mood," and to the mediacy that Stanzel sees as a defining feature of narrative itself.[24] Although I see no need to treat the author as a narrator, Plato is like a narrator (and, in the *Republic*, Socrates is one) who controls information in ways that both deny and fuel our desire for complete and ultimate knowledge.[25] The very fact that Plato's distance from speech in the dialogues needs somehow to be explained indicates its modalizing force; if, that is, I am right that interpreters must explain this distance away in order to reconstruct a subtext of univocal Platonic assertions.

Local Qualification in Socratic Dialogue

Most of what interests me about modality in the current study is a matter of semantic interpretation that extends well beyond the sentence. Some of the most important modalizing structures, such as fictionality and narrativity, are

---

[22] See also Lamarque and Olsen 1994:321–338; cf. Cohn 2001:489.
[23] Nightingale 2002 (epistemological distance) and 2004:96 (rhetoric of estrangement); Rowe 2007:25, 28–32; McCabe 2008:103–106; Clay 2000:28, 37; see also Tigerstedt 1977:94.
[24] Genette 1980:162–185; Stanzel 1984:6.
[25] For other views of narrative in Plato, see Morgan 2004 and Halliwell 2009.

discursive and global rather than sentential and local, lying far outside the usual scope of linguistics but lending themselves to literary-rhetorical analysis. Yet the *Republic*, and the dialogues generally, are permeated by modalizing expressions at all levels of description, so much so that modalization might well be called a defining feature of Plato's depictions of Socratic dialogue.[26] A promising way to understand modalization in Plato might be to focus on the amorphous phenomenon known as Socratic irony. I think my argument here, however, will be better served by focusing on linguistic features that are relatively unambiguous. Continuing to draw on concepts from the scientific realm of linguistics for the nonscientific purposes of humanistic interpretation, we may identify specific as well as broad indicators of discursive modality in the language of Plato's text.

As a rule, conversation lends itself to specific grammatical constructions, and it becomes even more idiosyncratic in Plato's portrayal of exchanges dominated by Socrates. Some general and commonplace modalizing expressions are ubiquitous and accentuated enough to be eminently familiar to readers of Plato's dialogues. These include statements explicitly qualified by various lexical elements; questions, commands, and exhortations; and hypothetical conjectures, proposals, conditions, and forecasts. All of these constructions may be distinguished from straightforward declarative statements made in the indicative mood: they are forms of expression that do not communicate ideas, things, and situations as they are, but instead tender possibilities for consideration, describing what could or should be. Before undertaking a closer analysis of textual details in subsequent chapters, it will be worthwhile to survey briefly some of the ways that Plato's dialogues, and the *Republic* in particular, are unusually saturated with expressions of possibility. As in English, modal expressions in Greek are often genteel and laden with potential irony. But the main function under consideration here is the sense of remoteness—the perspectival mediation of certainty, fact, and reality—that can accumulate under the weight of nondeclarative forms of speech.

The conversation between Socrates and his companions is predominantly clever, urbane, teasing, and polite, and its casual tone creates another dimension of constant qualification. Elements of this tone, such as wordplay, contribute to a small-scale tendency toward digression that resembles the distractibility of real-life speakers in casual conversation. Along with particles, which are used in myriad and virtually untranslatable ways (and many of which could be labeled modalizing particles), the text is thoroughly peppered with polite expressions

---

[26] On the model of linguistics, levels of description here correspond to categories or dimensions of constituents, as in the level of words, phrases, or sentences.

of conversational modesty.[27] Of these, I would single out some verbs for special notice: *horaō* 'to see' (used of following the conversation, as in "I see [what you mean]"); *dokeō* 'to think, seem' (often used with the dative case to express an opinion, as in "it seems to me"); and *phainō* 'to make appear' (often used in the passive, conceding likelihood in terms of appearance rather than reality, as in "it appears"). These commonplace words, which act as incidental stitches holding the conversation together, reappear in consciously heuristic discussion as crucial topics: appearance, opinion, likeness, and reality. Such verbs are liberally supplemented by conversational expressions of likelihood, necessity, and truth—including *isōs* 'perhaps'; *eikos* 'likely, probable'; *dei* 'it is necessary'; *khrē* 'it must'; *anankē* 'necessarily'; *alēthē* 'true'.

Given Socrates' obsession with questioning through conversation, a text such as the *Republic* naturally contains an extraordinary quantity of questions. Questioning is thus a foregrounded linguistic phenomenon in the text. It is also sometimes a debated topic in the conversation, as when Thrasymachus accuses Socrates of being an avid questioner but an evasive answerer (336c–338a). Some questions in the dialogue function as statements, others are really responses to questions, but the tone of questioning is often relentless. Imperatives of various sorts are also obviously much more prevalent in the conversation of the *Republic* than in, say, the nonfictional, historical prose of Thucydides. Characters urge themselves and the conversation forward in various indirect ways. "Is it resolved [*dokei*] that we must [*khrēnai*] try to carry this out?" asks Socrates at one point, questioning whether the group's inquiry should continue, adding "I suppose [*oimai*] it's no small job, so consider it" (δοκεῖ οὖν χρῆναι ἐπιχειρῆσαι περαίνειν; οἶμαι μὲν γὰρ οὐκ ὀλίγον ἔργον αὐτὸ εἶναι: σκοπεῖτε οὖν, 369b). While the legislative "is it resolved?" (*dokeō*) has a ring of decisiveness, the obligation of "must" (*khrē*) is softened by "try," which prioritizes effort over success. Similarly, the resolution to accept the obligation is proposed in a question rather than declared outright. Then "I suppose" qualifies the litotes of "no small job" with an ironic recognition of the difficulty involved, and the imperative "consider it" offers the interlocutor Adeimantus a chance to back out. Along with commands (which are usually in the imperative mood), we have many hortatory uses of the subjunctive serving a similar function, particularly in the first-person plural. "Let us make [*poiōmen*] a city-state in discourse from the beginning" is a typically phrased Socratic exhortation (τῷ λόγῳ ἐξ ἀρχῆς ποιῶμεν πόλιν, 369c).

In their discussion of ideas and methods, the characters in the *Republic* spin out all manner of speculation: conjectures, provisional plans, and hypothetical scenarios (sequences of imaginary events constructed from nonasserted

---

[27] On particles and qualification, see Cook 1996:139–155.

premises or conditions). Grammatically, these speculative ventures rely heavily on the optative mood. This question asked by Socrates is an interesting example:

εἰ γιγνομένην πόλιν θεασαίμεθα λόγῳ, καὶ τὴν δικαιοσύνην αὐτῆς ἴδοιμεν ἂν γιγνομένην καὶ τὴν ἀδικίαν;

"If we should watch [*theasaimetha*] a city-state coming into being in discourse, ... would we also see [*idoimen*] its justice coming into being, and its injustice?"

369a

For now, suffice it to observe that this overdetermined sentence may be read as a methodological, conditional, speculative, and rhetorical question. Having the force of a conditional statement, it describes a possible state of affairs: if one should do this, one would do that. At the same time, with the force of a question, the sentence outlines a possible course of action, taking on the guise of a proposal, an exhortation, and a supposition that could be accepted. The hypothesis is a theoretical possibility that could, in turn, be accepted as a practical possibility.

In traditional grammars of ancient Greek, the should–would construction just observed is known as the future-less-vivid and is classified as a future or potential condition. There is a sense in which the lack of commitment in such conditional sentences already makes them function like questions; they are limited to proposing possibilities. As Goodwin writes in his standard reference work on *Greek Moods and Tenses*, "the question as to the fulfillment of the future condition is still undecided."[28] Hence, in analyzing the example just discussed, we may refer to the possibility raised by the conditional if-clause (we might watch); the possibility of fulfillment in the then-clause (we might see); and the possibility, raised by the question, of accepting the entire statement as a supposition for further reasoning (we might agree). And let us not forget that the future is, strictly speaking, always unknown. As a modern linguist puts it, "in general, everything which relates to the future is *qualitate qua* hypothetical, since a possible rather than the actual world is involved."[29] The future-less-vivid conditional sentence in ancient Greek is thus named because it emphasizes

---

[28] Goodwin 1890, sec. 392.

[29] Wakker 1994:21. So Comrie 1985 notes that the future tense is "necessarily more speculative" than the past, "in that any prediction we make about the future might be changed by intervening events" (43). For more on tenses and modality see Fleischman 1989. Quirk et al. suggest that the future tense does not really exist in English, and see the verb form *will* as essentially a modal auxiliary (1972:84–90).

possibility over likelihood. But even expressions of likelihood (or plausibility) remain modalized (remote from certainty) to a significant degree.[30]

Indeed, the modality and temporality of making a city-state in discourse is more complex than it might at first appear. When planning city-states and their governments in the *Republic*, Socrates and his companions often use predictive, future-oriented constructions in ways that signal the theoretical force of their conversational practice. For example: "The farmer, as it seems, won't make [*poiēsetai*] his own plow himself," says Socrates at one point (ὁ γὰρ γεωργός, ὡς ἔοικεν, οὐκ αὐτὸς ποιήσεται ἑαυτῷ τὸ ἄροτρον, 370c). Even this apparently simple statement about an imaginary farmer is both a proposal for the city-state and a suppositional description of what would happen in the proposed city-state if it were ever made. Because Socrates' proposal is looking for agreement, the sentence is also questioning; declarative rather than interrogative or conditional in form, but questioning and hypothetical in function. The sentence also happens to be qualified ("as it seems") and negative ("won't make"), features that further modalize its force. Meanwhile, because the speakers are making a plan rather than an actual city-state, what they are doing in the present (in the practice of actual conversation) keeps getting thrown into the future (toward the possibility of action). "We will also need traders," remarks Socrates, for instance (καὶ ἐμπόρων δὴ δεησόμεθα, 371a). The plan needs traders in the present, but the planners would need traders if they actually were to make their city-state in the future.

Conditional constructions, which present one proposition as being dependent on (and thus subordinated under) another, are especially important for the interpretation elaborated in the second half of this book. Plato's Socrates is fond of building elaborate sequences of argumentation that rest on hypothetical foundations. In grammar, where "a declarative main clause typically conveys the speaker's commitment to the truth of the proposition expressed, such a commitment is often lost under subordination" (CGEL 174); even a statement like *I know he is ill* does not have the same force as *he is ill*. If there is indeed "a significant association between subordination and markers of modality" (CGEL 174), this is only compounded when an introductory main verb is itself explicitly modal in meaning (*I doubt he is ill*). My point here, though, is that the modalizing role of grammatical subordination can shed light on a related phenomenon in Socratic discourse, seen in theoretical experiments performed by way of words that accrete to form expansive chains of interdependent argument.

---

30 Scalar models of linguistic modality that measure degrees of remoteness from actuality are comparable with some philosophical theories of conditionals: "Conditionals can be accepted with different degrees of closeness to certainty" in "a range of epistemic attitudes" (Edgington 2008, sec. 3.1); see Ramsey 1990:145–163.

In one basic pattern found in the *Republic*, interdependent claims (themselves often put forth as proposals, rather than firm assertions) derive from and refer back to a suppositional ground that is decidedly unasserted. When this happens, the hypothetical modality of the initial supposition can cast a persistent attitude of uncertainty over subsequent claims and conclusions.

Global Modality in the *Republic*

All of the modalizing features just described, which are common enough in ancient Greek but endemic to Plato's dialogues, accumulate in the back-and-forth of conversation, forming an important aspect of Platonic style by saturating the text with modal expressions. If the *Republic* as a whole does not come across as modalized by these local instances of qualified speech, this is largely because the conversation in the book has a strong heuristic pulse that propels it through compelling arguments and thematic statements. No matter how modalized it may be, these statements of opinion undoubtedly whet readers' desire to possess a linear Socratic-Platonic message. For the *Republic* portrays the evolution of a conversation from disorientation and aimless small talk into a self-conscious project, in which the speakers adopt methods for the purpose of understanding justice and injustice, and these topics are treated as objects to be pursued, seen, and found. At the same time, however, the discourse of this heuristic project is globally modalized by tropes that rhetorically establish distance between the seekers and their goals. Where an interpretation focused on expository, linear argumentation in the text might insist that this is Plato's *real* meaning—that the book's pattern of distancing is meant to replace the conversation's pattern of methodical seeking—the second half of my study observes that these are major dimensions of the *Republic* that both exist concurrently *and* have contradictory functions. In other words, a strong current of methodological self-examination (a countercurrent, if you like) accompanies the heuristic arguments found in the book, articulating a perspective in which fixed conclusions keep turning into ongoing questions.

Recursion is the master trope, if you will, driving this thematic countercurrent. For instance, the way that the *Republic*'s conversational investigation of justice keeps doubling back on itself, becoming a conversation *about* the investigation of justice, is a major example of recursion in the text. We see recursion when a version of something occurs within itself, a phenomenon that can reach the extreme of infinite regression known as a *mise-en-abîme*. Here is how Jorge Luis Borges describes the famous literary example of the *Thousand and One Nights*, in which virtually countless narratives are embedded within each other: "This collection of fantastic tales duplicates and reduplicates to the point of

vertigo the ramifications of the central story in later and subordinate stories"
(1964:195). The *Republic*, I would stress, is permeated by similarly embedded
structures of regressive self-reflection.[31]

Thematically, recursion in the *Republic* tends to emphasize the difficulties
faced by human beings who are asking questions about the highest forms of
knowledge. The closer the inquiry gets to talking about its highest goals, the
more those goals are seen to recede from the seekers' grasp. My analysis of the
text will give special attention to interrelated varieties of recursion, notably
fictionality, digression, reported speech, and hypothetical speculation. These
are large-scale tropes that work in sequences of subordination—so subsequent
events in a fictional narrative remain under the auspices of fictional premises; a digression is subordinate to a main topic; a report is subordinate to an
original; and a speculative proposal is subordinate to a supposition. As recursive sequences (a digression in a digression in a digression, for instance), these
tropes amplify modality by extending and persisting through longer stretches
of text. The next three chapters consider different sequences: the *Republic* as
a fictional narrative, the conversational inquiry into the ideal state, and the
discussion of the Good as an ideal object of knowledge. In these sequences I
discern a recursive, self-reflective, and modalizing perspective on methodical
investigation that pervades the book as a whole.

---

[31] For more on the *mise-en-abîme* (a phrase drawn from heraldry by André Gide), see Dällenbach
1989; see also Bal 2009:62–64, who prefers to call such narratives "mirror-texts."

Part 2

Concerning the *Republic*

4

From Beginning to End and Back Again

WHEN READING AN EXPOSITORY WORK of heuristic inquiry and argumentation, we can take it as a given that the work itself relies on an
underlying framework of methodical progress toward an endpoint, a destination. This assumption does not apply to the *Republic*, however, mainly because
the book is not a heuristic inquiry but a depiction of one. We still desire to
reach a destination, but the methodical progression of conversation, embedded
in a narrative, participates in an intellectualized sort of plot.[1] This part of my
study argues that, unlike the inquiry pursued by the characters in it, one of the
primary functions of the *Republic*'s conceptual and rhetorical infrastructure is
to express uncertainty.

As a long text about an extended conversation, the *Republic* goes a long
distance before reaching an elliptical conclusion. A huge array of opinions and
sayings are entertained during the course of the book, beliefs that range from
familiar platitudes to outrageous perversions of archaic and classical Greek
thought, and these beliefs are attributed to a vast range of sources. In Plato's
presentation of these opinions a thoroughgoing and insistent distance evinces
an attitude of ongoing curiosity and experimentation rather than settled
certainty. To put an even sharper, negative edge on this point, the *Republic*'s
portrayal of method can be coherently understood as a renunciation of authorial authority, a repudiation of human complacency, and a refusal to settle for
and on an (inadequate) telos or stopping point. The pattern I am drawing attention to, however, is neither skeptical, pessimistic, panironic, nor panaporetic
but rather experimental, curious, and intrepid; combining exploration (at times

---

[1]   In this study, the term *embedded* does not have the sense reserved for describing narrative levels
(e.g. Genette 1980:46). Borrowing linguistic terms related to recursion, I am simply referring to
the occurrence of one structural element inside another. Also, the superordinate structure may
be said to contain and dominate the subordinate structure, without necessarily being resumed
later like a kind of framing device. In my reading, Socrates' narrative in the *Republic* contains
the previous day's conversation and persists through it without ever leaving off or resuming,
while the conversation in turn contains other structures, and so on. For relevant terms used in
linguistics, see Trask 2007, s.vv. "recursion," "embedding," "nesting," and "descendant."

immoderate) with an awareness of human inadequacy.[2] Plato submits possibilities for our consideration, in a literary form that propels intellectual exploration onward, unhindered by premature certainties no more than by doubts.

As I see it, the *Republic* offers an interesting and sustained reflection on method. Plato's book describes and examines the methods pursued by Socrates and his companions in the course of the long conversation that dominates it. The book's recursive structure may be described as follows: the casual conversation (conversational discourse) is embedded in Socrates' narrative (narrative discourse), and the heuristic investigation (methodical discourse) is embedded in the conversation. Thus the book is not just about topics such as justice; its subject matter is also methodological: the book is *about* the conduct of (philosophical) conversation and inquiry. In this way, the *Republic* is a remarkably and strangely self-aware and self-critical text. And this strangeness, furthermore, is reflected in an outlandish view of method. Whereas *conventional* methods of inquiry—for Plato as for us—are understood to reach their goals, seeking to reach and hold fixed positions, the *Republic* reflexively explores the possibility that philosophy is perhaps better viewed as an ongoing, unending exploration of possibilities.

One might see the *Republic* shifting attention from the content of arguments to the conduct of argumentation, but I find it more accurate to observe that the conduct of argument (method) is repeatedly and recursively turned into the content of the discussion. At bottom, such a view is made possible by a corresponding shift on the part of the reader from a focus on the *what* of the text to a literary-rhetorical focus on the *how*. The discussion of literary form in the previous half of this study shows that literary form, as it is perceived by scholars today, designates those aspects of the text that do not directly communicate authorial propositions. Having multiple speakers share ideas in a setting described by a narrator, for instance, is literary insofar as it is not a direct expression of the author's opinions. By the same token, the resulting mitigation of authorial commitment is, as I have suggested, a serviceable indicator of literariness. Given this negative delimitation of literary form, flipping it around clears the way for a claim that is, in effect, the opposite of the teleological explanation: a primary function of literary form in the *Republic* is precisely to establish distance between author and text, between Plato and what he wrote. Although readers have traditionally resisted going along with Plato's manifest elusiveness, primarily because they want to reach a Platonic telos, the *Republic* may be seen to suggest reasons why a radical questioning of teleological

---

[2] For different views of Plato's open-endedness, see Rowe 2007:20–25; Blondell 2002:4–14; Rutherford 1995:25–29; Reeve 1988:xii; Tigerstedt 1977:92–107, with Stefanini 1949:xxvii–lviii.

methodology might be in order in the pursuit of higher ideas. Which is to say that, although my argument depends on a shift in interpretive perspective, this shift is motivated by Plato's text, which itself directs a great deal of attention toward the conduct of argumentation, to the point where methodological questions become a matter of content.

The Topos of the Path and the Topic of Method

In the *Republic*, as in modern linguistics, the notion we now call *modality* is generally conceptualized in terms of physical and temporal distance (remoteness). A good first step in interpreting modality in the *Republic* is to consider the topos (in the literary sense of "commonplace") of the *path* as it figures throughout the dialogue. "Like the *Odyssey*, the *Republic* is an extended journey," observes Jacob Howland, suggesting that the dialogue not only describes a philosophical journey but also is itself a dynamic path of words and ideas.[3] The journey plays a prominent and versatile role in the text; it is a richly significant (overdetermined) metaphorical and conceptual figure, and my point here is that a major function of this figure is to evoke the theme of method.[4]

Paths of discourse and of thought are fundamental metaphors in ancient Greek from early on, and they are rampant in Plato's works.[5] Throughout the *Republic*, many different types of movement, including Socrates' physical trip to the Piraeus, are formulated as paths: procedures of conversation and argumentation, which the conversationalists describe as paths; specific methods of reasoning, such as the path of dialectic; the descent and ascent of the philosopher king and of the prisoners in the cave scenario; and the journey of the soul in the tale of Er. Each of these paths contributes to the text's emphasis on methodology and its interest in questions of procedure, while the characters strive to investigate profound but elusive ideals. The prevalence of paths running through the *Republic* encourages readers to view the entire work as both a digressive path and a self-referential discourse; it is a narrative path about paths.

The text itself, like the conversation that Socrates describes in his retrospective narrative, can be construed as a figurative *hodos* 'path, road, way; journey', and this metaphor is a major verbal element in the book's preoccupation with

---

[3]   Howland 2004:48. Among other traits that he associates with different ancient literary genres that inform the *Republic*, Howland notes "antidogmatic openness" and "critical self-awareness." These characteristics are particularly germane to my view of the journey as a rhetorical matrix of self-criticism.

[4]   See also Schur 1998.

[5]   See Becker 1937 and Snell 1955, ch. 13.

method (*methodos* 'path [*hodos*] of pursuit [*meta-*]'). Accordingly, characteristics of the figurative path are also major themes throughout the book. These include aspects of distance and direction that readily apply to methods of searching as well as to the journey taken by the characters in the narrative. Indeed, the design of Plato's text makes it notably difficult to distinguish the figurative from the literal journey, since conversation is the means by which the characters do their seeking (just as the same word, *dialegomai* 'to converse', is used for both dialogue and dialectic). In the conversation led by Socrates, the verb *dierkhomai* 'to go through' is regularly used to designate discussion, conceptualizing talking as traveling. The goals or ends of this investigative journey are portrayed as distant, remote, and difficult to reach.[6] One way to talk about the difficulties encountered by interpreters of Plato's dialogue form is to focus on Plato's treatment of conversation as a meandering journey.

Not surprisingly, frequent instances of self-reflection may take much of the credit for slowing the search down and leading it off course. Such pauses are clearly meant to make the conversation more methodical—better directed toward success. The same may be said for the conversation's frequent and frequently self-conscious digressions, deferrals, postponements, detours, and evasions. At one point, when Socrates observes that "a rather *lengthy* stage of argument has been *gone through* [*diexelthontes*]" (καὶ οἱ μὴ διὰ μακροῦ τινος διεξελθόντες λόγου), Glaucon replies, "perhaps that's because it could not easily have been done through a *short* one" (ἴσως γάρ, ἔφη, διὰ βραχέος οὐ ῥάδιον, 484a). Glaucon's casual and provisional contrast between methods associates difficulty with the short (*brakhus*) route and accomplishment with the long (*makros*) one. Sometimes, he is suggesting, a detour is the best way to reach your goals, thus avoiding impediments and impasses. But a significant rhetorical (formal-semantic) pattern in the text shows that while methodically adopting evasive maneuvers does keep the conversation going, it simultaneously leads the conversation away from where it was headed. Noticing this pattern is very different from picking at a flaw in the logic of an argument; my point has to do with how ideas and words interact in a specific text, and not with something that Plato has supposedly done wrong. Because the conversational method keeps turning by way of self-reflective passages that result in further turning, an overdetermining cascade of digression emphasizes the distance of goals that are continually displaced by provisional findings.

---

6   The conversation's length and difficulty are acknowledged at, e.g., 348b, 354b–357a, 369b, 376d, 435d, 450a, 484a, 504c–d, 506d, 615a.

The Beginning of the Story

By examining the beginning and the end of Plato's text, we may gain a sense of the *Republic's* global sweep, in contradistinction to the arc of the conversation that monopolizes the book once it gets going. Looking at the whole in this manner, the text may be read as a map of two routes taken simultaneously, one traced by the practice of conversation (which rises to the height of theory), the other by theoretical argumentation (which is brought down by the human limitations of conversational practice). The contrast I emphasize here is simply between the conversation and the book. Because the book contains the conversation while the conversation tends to reflect on itself, the conversation is subordinate to the book and the whole is deeply self-reflective. The participants in the conversation develop theories and make arguments, seeking to reach fixed intellectual goals that include a definition of justice and a defense of its inherent desirability, a sketch of the ideal *politeia*, and a curriculum for the education of guardians. As presented in the book, however, these are not simply argumentative steps that fall short when dissected; they are cognitive steps mediated, modalized, performed, and deformed in the language of the text.

It is worth thinking of the beginning of the *Republic* as a premise. Not a theoretical premise, but the premise that we must accept in order to read on. The beginning describes for us an imaginary situation that establishes preconditions for what will follow.[7] Plato, in effect, asks his audience to imagine Socrates recounting this story out loud to a group of listeners. In setting this scene, Plato's establishment of Socrates' narrative is the first stage, the first condition, in a vertiginous cascade of reported speech. With great complexity, instances of reported speech are nested within each other throughout the *Republic*. In a recursive fashion, each embedded report is subordinated to another, starting with Plato's beginning the dialogue. If we agree with the conditions established by the initial scenario, in which Socrates narrates the story of a conversation that took place yesterday—and the text gives us every opportunity to accept this premise as agreeable—then this fictional point of departure assumes a structurally dominant position in the lengthy verbal pattern of subordination that is the text of the *Republic*. But this dominance (which is, moreover, casual and circumstantial in its initial recollection of events leading up to the long conversation) is challenged by continual changes of topic, perspective, and

---

[7] "The beginning of a work of art must also in a sense be its definition, since it acts like a frame to set that work apart from others and to enclose it as a single thing in itself" (Ford 1992:18). Endings can have a similarly global impact: "The sense of a beginning ... must in some important way be determined by the sense of an ending" (P. Brooks 1984:94). See also Said 1975 and Kermode 1967.

procedure.[8] Moreover, when we begin to read the *Republic*, we are faced with a narrative, rightly renowned for its philosophical content, in which neither expository content nor literary exposition (i.e. the subject matter; what the text is about) is particularly evident. The ensuing search for a dominant and stable subject matter would presumably proceed regardless of whether the text was considered a dogmatic treatise or a literary narrative. Just as each subsequent part of the *Republic* is subordinated to a larger context of ongoing conversation, so each change in course is perceived as a digression, a deviation from an established norm of structure and meaning. The sequence of digressions is so elaborate, prominent, and pervasive in the *Republic* as to bring the topic of digression into the foreground of the reading experience.

Although most readers fully recognize the episodic, incidental quality of the *Republic*'s beginning, it is worth noting the pronounced way in which Plato immediately opens up room for questions of authority and relevance, regarding who is speaking and what the point of this document might be. One of the challenges of the *Republic* from the start is to figure out what the text is about. What is its subject matter? Where is this book going as we begin to read it? These questions try to get at something essential regarding the book as a whole, as an integral text.

I would start with two responses. In the first place, the *Republic* has the form of a narrated dialogue, and the entire narrative traces the development of a conversation. Socrates begins by telling us how the conversation got started, and he continues to recount the trajectory of that conversation for the duration of the book. If, in the manner of classical narrative theory, we separate out the aspects of *story* ("the narrated events, abstracted from their disposition in the text and reconstructed in their chronological order, together with the participants in these events") and *discourse* (the telling of those events, arranged to exhibit a plot that typically exhibits causality), the story of the *Republic* is a conversation-event.[9] The conversation is the *what* that the text invites readers to imagine to have happened.

Second, the conversation is outlandishly long and exceptionally wide in scope. Justice, education, mimesis, truth, and philosophy are a few of the great abstractions that this conversation is about. Although it is easy to single out one topic and give it precedence, and even to proclaim that a conclusive understanding of that topic has been reached, the book does not make this claim. Instead, the topic of the book is a constantly moving target, while at the same

---

[8] On dominance and subordination of discourse types, see Jakobson 1987:41–49 ("The Dominant"), 69; Cohn 1999:12–13; Blondell 2002:37–38.

[9] Rimmon-Kenan 1983:3; see also Genette 1980:25–32 and Prince 2003a s.v. "story." For a brief historical overview of narrative theory, see Prince 2003b.

time Socrates' compulsion to interrogate his companions and their ideas gives the conversation a frequently renewed sense of orientation toward an ultimate ideal. Socrates' interest in searching with others tends toward a single ideal of philosophical illumination (as in the Good), a goal that would ultimately include and subsume all other topics of conversation if it were ever found.

According to the Oxford English Dictionary, to *digress* is "to go aside or depart from the course or track; to diverge, deviate, swerve." The most common sense is "to deviate from the subject in discourse or writing." As the word *from* in these definitions indicates, digression is necessarily a relative concept. One needs first to have an established norm, a subject understood as a direction or orientation, from which to deviate. Digression is also conceived of as a highly metaphorical procedure. Discourse—in this instance, the written course followed by the reader—is a kind of topic-path. And digression is a turning whereby that path of words diverges from whatever topic is considered proper to it. It is no accident that the *Republic* is saturated with metaphors that evoke this conceptual network, linking physical travel with paths of inquiry, conversation, and discourse—and with the metaphysical journey of souls after death.

While the *hodos* operates as a plurisignificant figure that is demonstrably prevalent in the text of the *Republic*, concomitant notions of distance, direction, and position naturally characterize the different kinds of path represented in the book. It would not be an exaggeration to point out that the path (of movement, words, and thought) is an extraordinary metaphor. For one thing, the language of the path informs Western conceptions of method and justice: both may be straight, correct, justified—or mistaken, deviant, crooked, off-target, and beside the point. The concept of deviation (turning) from the straight path is also crucial to how we think about metaphor and rhetoric (troping).[10] And the notion of distance is likewise fundamental to the metalanguage used by linguists, but familiar to us all, to describe temporal and modal remoteness.[11] In these respects, the path is a metaphor of metaphors and a trope of tropes, which makes it especially suitable for self-reflection. The figure is conceptually pregnant—structurally and rhetorically overdetermined—by definition, if you will. We cannot conceive of movement along a path without entering a vast network of dead metaphors that express relations of distance and direction. And although we may discuss these paths as metaphors, they were already just as literalized in ancient Greek as they are in many modern languages. Such

---

[10] Examples are also discussed in the *Republic*. For instance, Adeimantus quotes Hesiod to the effect that virtue "is a long road, rough and steep" (ὁδὸν μακράν τε καὶ τραχεῖαν, 364c–d).

[11] Fleischman 1989, Comrie 1985. See also discussions of tense and modality in CGEL 2002:173–174 and Palmer 1986:208–218.

metaphors can, when noticed or reanimated, put great pressure on the conventional separation of literal from metaphorical.

Many conceptual terms of importance to the current study, here accompanied by etymological glosses concerning motion, bear mentioning: *method* (pursuing by path), *trope* (turning), *version* (turning), *topic* (staying in place), *discourse* (running about, conversing), *conversation* (turning around), *recursion* (running back), *digression* (stepping aside), *degradation* (stepping down), *evasion* (going away), *metaphor* (carrying beyond), *report* (carrying back), *investigation* (tracking footprints), *stance* (standing), *distance* (standing apart), and *term* (marking a limit)—all such terms and concepts return to the notion of a path and its turnings.

The Beginning of the Text

So the concept of travel is inseparable from our understanding of method, and it emerges at the start of the *Republic* in a disorienting series of turns that make it especially difficult to tell where the book is going and when it is digressing. Beginning with "I went down," we are confronted by an anonymous narrator, later identified as Socrates, telling us about a journey he took the day before.

> <u>κατέβην</u> χθὲς εἰς Πειραιᾶ μετὰ Γλαύκωνος τοῦ Ἀρίστωνος προσευξόμενός τε τῇ θεῷ καὶ ἅμα τὴν ἑορτὴν βουλόμενος <u>θεάσασθαι</u> τίνα <u>τρόπον</u> ποιήσουσιν ἅτε νῦν πρῶτον <u>ἄγοντες</u>. καλὴ μὲν οὖν μοι καὶ ἡ τῶν ἐπιχωρίων <u>πομπὴ</u> ἔδοξεν εἶναι, οὐ μέντοι ἧττον ἐφαίνετο πρέπειν ἣν οἱ Θρᾷκες <u>ἔπεμπον</u>.

> "I went down [*katebēn*] yesterday to the Piraeus with Glaucon, the son of Ariston, to pray to the Goddess, and also because I wished to see [*theasasthai*] the manner [*tropon*] in which they would manage the festival, since they were now conducting [*agontes*] it for the first time. I thought the march [*pompē*] of the citizens very fine, but it was no more respectable than how the Thracian contingent marched [*epempon*]."

> 327a

As other scholars have noted, the descent denoted by the dialogue's first word (*katebēn* 'I went down') inaugurates a rich thematic network of descents (and ascents) that run through the entire work, and this first mention of a journey is certainly crucial to the present study.[12] To mention some of the most striking parallels, Socrates' physical catabasis to the port of Athens is echoed in the

---

[12] See e.g. McPherran 2010:1, Jacobs 2008:45, Smith 2007:3, Clay 1992:125–129, Brann 2004:116–121.

scenario of the cave and in the tale of Er, which are central and concluding parts of the book respectively.[13] Insofar as Socrates starts by heading homeward, his Odyssean journey returns to a new beginning at the end of the text, and the book's central pattern of progress as a turning to philosophy (518c–d) is modalized by a circular pattern that becomes recursive in the final pattern of cyclical reincarnation with which the book concludes.[14]

The importance of the path as a concept is reinforced by several other words in this opening passage. Socrates says that he went to the festival for two reasons, prayer and spectacle. His report emphasizes the latter, focusing on the topic of *tropos* 'turn, manner, way' in his concern for the "manner" of presentation at the festival. He went to see how people would lead (*agō* 'to lead, conduct') or conduct (*pempō* 'to send, conduct, escort') their processions. On a small scale, Socrates leads us into the narrative by describing a physical journey whose purpose is to watch (*theaomai* 'to behold, view') how some very small physical journeys proceed. And again, on a very small scale, this pattern (a journey to see the progress of a journey) anticipates the parallel journey of conversation, a journey of words that will frequently look back, self-reflexively and self-critically, on its own process. The book will end with another sort of prayer. In the course of the narrative, the initial spectacle will come to seem trivial, but precisely because it is positioned in the foreground, from which it will recede, when seen in retrospect it becomes a mock spectacle, a foil for the more important conversational effort to seek, see, and proceed methodically.[15] Socrates reports nothing else about this first (daytime) festival, so that in terms of the narrative, this first spectacle is merely a pretext for a chance meeting with Polemarchus. It will become easy to imagine that the long conversation takes the place of the soon-to-be-forgotten spectacle of a relay race and other nightlong sights (mentioned at 328a), just as the more cerebral journey of conversation will take precedence over physical action.[16] In yet another displacement, however, the conversation at Polemarchus' house, seen retrospectively, substitutes for a different conversation promised by Polemarchus: "After dinner we will get up and go out ... meet a lot of lads ... and talk [*dialexometha*]" (ἐξαναστησόμεθα γὰρ μετὰ τὸ δεῖπνον

[13] See Schur 1998, ch. 2; Howland 2004:43–46; Brann 2004, ch. 6.

[14] On the pedimental or ring structure of composition found in many of the dialogues, see Thesleff 2012 and Barney 2010, who discerns "a general pattern of explanatory regress" in the ring composition of the *Republic* (43).

[15] Nightingale 2004 makes clear the strong connection between the festival's spectacle and the Greek tradition of theoretical-metaphysical-philosophical speculation, whose semantic range is captured in the word *theoria* and related terms of vision associated with travel (esp. 74–83). See also Nagy 1990:164–165.

[16] Cf. Nightingale 2004:75.

καὶ τὴν παννυχίδα θεασόμεθα. καὶ συνεσόμεθά τε πολλοῖς τῶν νέων αὐτόθι καὶ <u>διαλεξόμεθα</u>, 328a).

The encounter with Polemarchus introduces several physical turns into the beginning of the narrative. Through a playfully elaborate turn of events, Socrates is led to change direction—and this physical turning is the first of the book's many digressions. The scene is described with considerable attention to the characters' spatial orientation, and the language here highlights the relative nature of movement in a particular direction. As the narrator tells us, he and Glaucon "were going away" (*apēimen*) "toward [*pros*] the city" (ἀπῇμεν <u>πρὸς</u> τὸ ἄστυ, 327b). The prefix *apo-* 'away from, back again' is the counterpart of the preposition *pros* 'toward'; the deictic function of these words depends on the viewpoint adopted by the speaker. The narrator continues, telling us that Polemarchus, seeing "from a distance" (*porrōthen*), perceived that the others were headed away, in the direction that the narrator calls "homeward" (*oikade*, κατιδὼν οὖν <u>πόρρωθεν</u> ἡμᾶς <u>οἴκαδε</u> ὡρμημένους, 327b).[17] To go away from the Piraeus is simultaneously to go toward the city; to go homeward is to go away from Polemarchus.

At this point in the text, Socrates has not yet been named—a fact that stands out all the more considering that we have been told where, why, when, and with whom he went. Paired with the homeward journey, this initial anonymity points up two different kinds of distance. One is simply the distance between a man, whose name is initially withheld in a manner that recalls the beginning of the *Odyssey*, and the goal of his journey, home.[18] As it happens, however, Socrates never reaches this goal in the *Republic*. The second remove is established by the mediation of narrative: Plato, unnamed in the text, has set up a narrator, initially also unnamed, who is describing the journey. Through the introduction of a single day's delay, Plato stresses our distance from the source of the story.[19]

Polemarchus sends a servant after our narrator, and the servant grabs the latter's cloak "from behind" (*opisthen*), so that he "turned round" (*metestraphēn*). Then, when the narrator asks the servant where Polemarchus is, Polemarchus' servant says "he is coming toward [*proserkhetai*] you from behind [*opisthen*]" (327b).[20] So the dynamic of movement in different directions is exaggerated by

---

[17] For Nightingale, "the notion of the distant viewer or viewpoint" is a major topic in Plato's work generally, and is explicitly addressed by the Stranger in the *Sophist* when he compares viewers who, looking from a distance (*porrōthen*, 234b), are deceived by visual images, to those who remain distant from the truth (234c) when listening to verbal imagery (2002:228). Cf. *Republic* 368d, discussed below.

[18] See Howland 2004 on the Odyssean implications of Socrates' journey.

[19] See Blondell 2002:17.

[20] κατιδὼν οὖν <u>πόρρωθεν</u> ἡμᾶς <u>οἴκαδε</u> ὡρμημένους Πολέμαρχος ὁ Κεφάλου ἐκέλευσε δραμόντα τὸν παῖδα περιμεῖναί ἑ κελεῦσαι. καί μου <u>ὄπισθεν</u> ὁ παῖς λαβόμενος τοῦ ἱματίου, κελεύει ὑμᾶς,

repetition. After reporting on the circumstances that led up to this meeting, the narrator reports on the meeting itself, and Polemarchus is now quoted saying pretty much what the narrator has already said: "Socrates, you seem to me to be heading away (*apiontes*) toward (*pros*) the city" (δοκεῖτέ μοι <u>πρὸς</u> ἄστυ ὡρμῆσθαι ὡς <u>ἀπιόντες</u>, 327c). The narrator seems to have taken his description of his own departure (which is earlier in the narrative discourse) from Polemarchus' spoken description of it (which follows in the discourse). It is therefore appropriate that the narrator's name emerges only when voiced by Polemarchus. The repetitions bring the story close to the discourse, but with enough interference to make the mediacy of narrative apparent. The direction of the narrative, in addition to the direction of the characters' movements, is foregrounded by a certain backwardness. And a character's discourse has been projected back into the narrator's, through a quirky sort of unattributed quotation.

Similar redundancy occurs in the description of the servant's actions. After the narrator describes how Polemarchus orders a servant to command Socrates to wait, the narrator then quotes the servant, who says, "Polemarchus commands you to wait" (κελεύει ὑμᾶς, ἔφη, Πολέμαρχος περιμεῖναι, 327b). In this brief description, the verb *keleuō* 'to command' thus occurs three times: first reported in the narrative (Polemarchus *commanded*), then quoted indirectly (Polemarchus *commanded* the servant *to command*), and then in a direct quotation of the command given by the servant. The exchange, as narrated, has the dynamic of a verbal relay race in which the participants are running into each other. When addressed by the servant from behind, Socrates turns around, and after acceding to Polemarchus and his crowd, Socrates goes "homeward" (*oikade*, 328b) once again, but this time he is headed to the house of Polemarchus and Cephalus in the Piraeus. Thus Socrates is reoriented, with the deictic word *oikade* indicating that he is in some sense going toward the same destination as before.

In summing up my analysis of this opening scene, I wish to discuss what these turnings have to do with rhetorical modalization. At this stage of the book, the journey being recounted is physical—it has not yet become a journey of words, let alone a metaphysical journey of contemplative vision (*theoria*) of the sort addressed in Andrea Nightingale's book *Spectacles of Truth in Classical Greek Philosophy* (2004). Yet even Socrates' journey homeward of yesterday is, by virtue of being recounted, pointedly mediated by Socrates' verbal narration. In this way, the journey's thematic significance (along with its distance and orientation) is reinforced by the verbal form of the narrative discourse: rhetorical

---

ἔφη, Πολέμαρχος περιμεῖναι. καὶ ἐγὼ <u>μετεστράφην</u> τε καὶ ἠρόμην ὅπου αὐτὸς εἴη. οὗτος, ἔφη, <u>ὄπισθεν προσέρχεται</u>. (327b)

digression in the narrative echoes the geographical detour that the narrative describes. More specifically, nested instances of reported speech have a recursive effect which corresponds verbally to the physical detour that takes Socrates from one direction to another. And the fictionality of the narrative introduces an uneasy tension between an imaginary conversation and the theoretical hypotheses it contains.

To adapt a literary-critical observation that Nightingale makes when discussing a related phenomenon in Plato's *Gorgias*, the opening stretch of narrative discourse in the *Republic* both foregrounds the theme of distance and enacts distancing effects.[21] Indeed, these phenomena are separable only in terms of an interpretive model. (Here it will again be helpful to distinguish story and discourse in the analysis of narrative.) In the story, Socrates' journey toward his goal is interrupted—and this interruption may be understood as a digression, a change of direction in the telling of the story. Rather than beginning with an account of an event, the narrative presents the festival as a nonevent, from which Socrates is departing. As I noted above, the festival is filtered by the narrator's retrospection, which treats it as a circumstantial false start whose eventfulness is defined by an unexpected change: Socrates is turned around and distracted from his homeward trajectory.

Narrativity and Fictionality

Interpreters of the dialogue as a whole are often inclined to view these introductory remarks, and indeed the entire first book of the *Republic*, as merely a sort of frame, separable from the ensuing philosophical arguments about justice, the city, and philosophy itself.[22] It is equally valid and formally correct, however, to observe that the narrator's voice (attitude, personality) is being established at the start, setting the tone for the whole book. Far from being a separable frame, this is an enduring voice (more overt at the start but always audible) that mediates the entire story.[23] In other words, the narrative situation (Socrates the narrator telling his story the day after the event) remains the same throughout the *Republic*, and does not act as a frame for a different, embedded, and autonomous narrative. (Other speakers do tell stories during the course of the long conversation. For example, Glaucon relates the story of the ring of Gyges, and

---

21 "Plato both dramatizes and thematizes the distance between earthly and cosmic vision" in the eschatological conclusion of his *Gorgias* (Nightingale 2002:238).

22 See Reeve's criticism of the interpretive myth underlying this approach (1988:xi). Clay 1992:115 rightly identifies the *Phaedo*, *Symposium*, *Theaetetus*, and *Parmenides*—and not the *Republic*—as "frame dialogues." See also Johnson 1998.

23 Speech tags ("he said," "I said") persist in the text of Socrates' narration as late as 614b, when they revert to tags within the tale told by Er.

Socrates the character tells the myth of Er.) Thus, in terms of the *Republic*'s form, the beginning is not a literary prologue to some other kind of separate discourse. Even though the setting fades from view as the book proceeds, the setting and the form of the narrative remain set, and the book does not manifestly shift from one form of discourse to another.

From the first word of the text, we know that someone is speaking in the first person. The tense of "I went down" (*katebēn*) separates the speaker in time from the event being described, while the following word ("yesterday") limits the temporal distance. After getting a taste of who and when, we learn where, what, and why (Piraeus, festival, to pray and watch)—all in the first sentence. This wealth of information, however, strikes a contrast with the delayed appearance of the narrator's name. Of course, we all know that Socrates is speaking, just as we all know that Odysseus is the "man" at the start of the *Odyssey*. Among other things, the delay in each instance draws attention to the identity of a well-known figure. Here, Socrates is *obviously* unidentified. Whether or not we already know (from experience or hearsay) that Socrates is speaking at the beginning of the *Republic*, the delay emphasizes the fact that it could be anyone, the first guess naturally falling on the author. In this way, the *Republic* immediately raises the question, "who is speaking?" And the answer ultimately functions as a pronounced and emphatic signal of fictionality: not the author. Herodotus and Thucydides, fittingly, start their histories with their own names.

The narrator immediately shares personal motivations and thoughts: he went to the new festival in order to pray, and to watch out of curiosity. His positive opinion of the Thracian performance is entirely subjective—in contrast with the epic poets, for instance, who never directly offer an opinion of their own like this one, that can be directly attributed to the speaker. Surely it would be bizarre to attribute this opinion to the author, Plato. Readers scarcely notice this opinion as one held by Socrates; even though it is the very first position our narrator takes, it quickly comes to seem incidental, contributing to the general impression of casualness.

Writing about ancient Greek fiction, J. R. Morgan makes the general point that "the necessary condition of fiction is that both sender and recipient are aware that it is factually untrue" (1993:180).[24] At the same time, fiction can and usually does contain plenty of facts that do correspond to the real world; for example, Socrates was a real person and the Piraeus was a real place. As Morgan points out, in the Greek novels of the third century C.E., "the represented world is, without exception, explicitly identified with reality" (198); a Greek novel cultivates verisimilitude: "a deliberately contrived pretense of historical

---

[24] So Larmarque and Olsen: "The fictive mode points away from belief" (1994:331).

authenticity" (200). But we may supplement the role of verisimilitude with a narratological account of fictional texts: "(1) its references to the world outside the text are not bound to accuracy; and (2) it does not refer exclusively to the real world outside the text."[25]

Insofar as the *Republic* is a work written by Plato and narrated by someone else, it is a work of fiction.[26] Socrates is a historical figure, but one who did not write dialogues and who was long dead by the time of Plato's writing. Plato has created an imaginary Socrates the narrator—not in the sense of having told a deceitful lie, and not in the sense of having devised a theoretical proposition, but also without claiming to report something that actually happened. The status of the historical figure Socrates in the *Republic* is comparable with that of Socrates in Aristophanes' *Clouds*, and of Napoleon in Tolstoy's *War and Peace*. The invented version of Socrates in the *Republic* is both a narrator and a character in the fictional narrative created by Plato. As a fictional narrative, the *Republic* creates a world that, while certainly referring to countless features of everyday human life on earth, has a book-bound existence. Morgan refers to a "contract of fictional complicity" (1993:187), and it is hard to believe that any competent reader, whether ancient or modern, has ever read the *Republic* without effortlessly entering into such a contract.[27] One of the many strange twists in the interpretation of Plato, twists occasioned by the strangeness of his writing, is the notion that the fictionality of a text such as the *Republic* is actually/really a fiction.

At the end of Book 1, when Socrates seems to have reached a desired conclusion, with even Thrasymachus conceding that justice is better than injustice, Socrates confesses that he has gone astray: instead of first figuring out what justice is, the question whether justice is more profitable than injustice distracted him: "I couldn't resist going [*elthein*] to this from that. So now the current outcome of our conversation [*dialogou*] is that I don't know anything" (οὐκ ἀπεσχόμην τὸ μὴ οὐκ <u>ἐπὶ τοῦτο ἐλθεῖν ἀπ' ἐκείνου</u>, ὥστε μοι νυνὶ γέγονεν ἐκ τοῦ <u>διαλόγου</u> μηδὲν εἰδέναι, 354b–c). The conversation has been inconclusive and (in a retrospective comment that mirrors Socrates' narration) has gone in a mistaken direction, resulting in one of Socrates' famous declarations

---

[25] Cohn 1999:15. See also Schaeffer 2009 on fictional narrative.

[26] See Genette 1993:54–84 and Cohn 1999:30–37 on this criterion: "As long as the speaker is named, on or within the text, and named differently from the author, the reader knows that one is not meant to take the discourse as a (referential) reality statement" (Cohn 1999:32). See also Gill 1993 and 1979 on fictionality in Plato.

[27] Morgan's contractual explanation of fiction brings to mind Philippe Lejeune's autobiographical pact (1989, ch. 1), which emphasizes the reader's reliance on paratextual or peritextual evidence in making the distinction between autobiography (which can contain lies) and fictional memoir. See also Mheallaigh 2008.

of ignorance. Despite Socrates' own hesitation and reluctance, however, the conversation itself keeps going. *The movement forward here is a function of digression.*

Toward an Ending of the Text

The ending of the *Republic*, featuring the embedded narrative commonly known as the Myth of Er, is itself lengthy and complex, building into an inspiring and dazzling jumble of bewildering, detailed ups and downs. A conclusion in which Socrates urges his listeners to journey forward into an afterlife that will never end, the ending of the *Republic* points beyond itself, in a gesture that exemplifies the book's strong tendency to render itself inconclusive. Stephen Halliwell makes a similar point: the book's final "vindication of justice looks clear enough at first sight," but it can also be seen to draw a "hermeneutic parallel" between our reading and the soul's survival, encouraging an endless cycle of interpretation that "Plato's text itself does not supply the means to bring to a definitive conclusion."[28] Without expecting the ending of the book to contain some sort of ultimate meaning, we may look there in order to see where the book was, is, and will always have been going. The ending of a book is, de facto, a destiny waiting for the reader, and it turns out that the ending of the *Republic* contains a glimpse of ultimate and enduring knowledge—knowledge reaching beyond death—after all. For mortals, all of whom must reckon with a destiny of death, the story of Er entertains the possibility of further turns on an endless roller coaster of a journey. With grand hopes accompanied by humor and whimsy, Socrates' fantastic description of death, destiny, and the afterlife provides the book with an ending about endings. And so, with this characteristically self-reflective gesture, the ending evinces the work's searching tenor and its marked tendency to frustrate readers' desire for closure. (For this very reason, those who wish to underplay the text's open-endedness will protest that the ending is precisely not characteristic of the rest of the work, that it is merely a digressive epilogue to the text rather than the ending of it.)[29]

The tale of Er, as recounted by Socrates (614a–621c), exhibits the major rhetorical types of distancing mentioned above. Expansive tropes—digression, reported speech, and hypothetical fiction—are closely intertwined in the way the tale, along with Socrates' concluding remarks, functions in the context of a conclusion. Just when the character Socrates might be expected (given his goal-oriented model of investigation) finally to offer a summation of his already

---

[28] Halliwell 2007:445–446. See also Halliwell 2011b, ch. 4, esp. 179–183; and 2011a.

[29] Grube and Reeve's comment at the beginning of Book 10: "The main argument of the *Republic* is now *complete*" (my emphasis).

scattered and highly qualified pronouncements concerning justice and the like, the text wrenches us out of our complacent familiarity with one fictional narrative (Socrates' tale about yesterday's conversation) and into yet another (Er's tale about the afterlife). For those scholars, including Julia Annas, who reconstruct the *Republic* into "a sustained defense of the thesis that justice is desirable in itself," this is a gross digression: "the myth is a lapse from the level of the main argument" (1981:349–350).

The narrative of Er is part of a recursive series that moves yet further from the plausible realism of a conversation between fictional-historical characters and into a fabulous world of increasingly anonymous hearsay. Socrates self-consciously stresses that his tale is not going to be "a tale of Alcinous" (Ἀλκίνου γε ἀπόλογον, 614b), referring to the proverbially lengthy embedded narrative by Odysseus at the court of the Phaeacians (*Odyssey* 9–12). But he is, in fact, about to present a rather lengthy, embedded narrative. For readers of the *Republic*, this reference by Socrates the character to a notably lengthy narrative reflects on the distance covered by the conversation being recounted by Socrates the narrator, while the famously embedded tale of Odysseus' fantastic wanderings may recall to us that the tale of Er is not just about Er, but also told by him.

After describing the rewards that accrue to the just man during life, Socrates prepares for the tale of Er (whose name is reminiscent of the Greek words for Eros and hero) with the following introductory remarks:

ταῦτα τοίνυν, ἦν δ' ἐγώ, οὐδέν ἐστι πλήθει οὐδὲ μεγέθει πρὸς ἐκεῖνα ἃ <u>τελευτήσαντα</u> ἑκάτερον περιμένει· <u>χρὴ</u> δ' αὐτὰ <u>ἀκοῦσαι</u>, ἵνα <u>τελέως</u> ἑκάτερος αὐτῶν ἀπειλήφῃ τὰ ὑπὸ τοῦ <u>λόγου</u> ὀφειλόμενα <u>ἀκοῦσαι</u>.

"In number and size," I said, "these are nothing in comparison with what awaits each one when he comes to an end [*teleutēsanta*]. One must [*khrē*] hear [*akousai*] these things, in order that each of those people may completely [*teleōs*] receive what is owed him by the discussion [*logos*] to hear [*akousai*]."

614a

These two sentences display a small-scale convergence of larger concerns that now await the reader: the text's completion, Socrates' effort to complete the conversation, and the soul's completion of a life. Although the verb *teleutaō* 'to come to an end' and the adverb *teleōs* 'completely' are both etymologically related to the noun *telos* 'end', the words as they occur here have no direct connection with each other. One can nevertheless observe a literary kind of interaction at work between them, which puts the discussion of death in a self-reflective perspective. Used intransitively, as here, the verb *teleutaō* connotes death; strictly speaking, what the just people come to the end of—life—is left unexpressed. The euphemism conveys less finality than would a verb such as *thnēskō* 'to die', for instance. And just so does this version of life's end leave the way open for the afterlife. If we were expecting a teleological view of death as the ultimate fulfillment of life, Socrates' eschatology will deny that death is a stopping point, thereby upending traditional notions of teleology.

Meanwhile, Socrates' emphasis on hearing (in the salient repetition of the verb *akouō*) maintains a self-conscious focus on the conduct of conversation. For the sake of clarity, I will call such conversational remarks *metaconversational* or *procedural* discourse.[30] This type of discourse is ubiquitous in the *Republic*, and it provides a running commentary that blends into the conversation, often attracting little notice. Commentary by Socrates the narrator is rare after the early stages of the book, but metaconversational comments by the conversationalists function in ways that merit comparison with more familiar modal functions of narratorial mediation.[31] My general point is that, once again, metaconversation is mixed up with the subject matter of the conversation, so that the subject matter of the *text* becomes recursive and is thereby modalized. While Socrates and Glaucon are indeed talking about the just man and his rewards, the text is reflecting on the conduct of the conversation.

This reflection happens in these two sentences in multiple ways. As just mentioned, the second occurrence of *akouō* 'to hear' stands out through repetition and potential redundancy. In the first instance, it is the group of conversationalists who must hear about the rewards that come after death, and it is through this hearing that the just may get what is owed to them (much as reputation is a form of hearsay). But the second reference to hearing, seemingly redundant, foregrounds a further point that Socrates is making about the conversation.[32] By extending the personification which has already turned an abstract concept (justice) into an individual representative (the just man), Socrates treats the just man as a listener who is present in the current conversation. Glaucon and the others must hear the tale of Er, but so too must the just man. And so not only does the conversation itself become a topic of conversation; inversely, a topic of the conversation (the just man) has become, rhetorically, a participant in it. He is now an embedded member of the conversation that conceived him. We may describe the just man's participation in the discussion that invented him as a peculiar kind of recursion, occasioned by rhetorical mirroring between conversational and metaconversational discourse.

---

[30] I borrow from a similar use of the term *procedural discourse* in Rose 1992.

[31] See Ferrari 2010 on Socrates as narrator.

[32] Adam (1902, *ad loc.*) defends the repetition of *akousai* as "welcome, if not necessary."

Socrates' main point is simply that the verbal account of the just man remains incomplete. Continuing a strand of metaphorical wordplay in which verbal accounts are part of a financial system of exchange (as at 612c; cf. 506e), the just are said to be "owed" an explanation that will tie up loose ends originally left by Socrates and Glaucon, a long way back, when external honors and rewards were excluded from the discussion in order to focus on justice in itself (358b). The financial metaphor is expanded and strengthened through another conflation of conversational conduct and subject matter: a parallel exists between two different kinds of rewards owed to just people after death; among the conversationalists, whose number now (figuratively) includes each of the just, getting the verbal explanation is (figuratively) a reward. Insofar as a verbal account is "owed" to each just man "by the conversation," the conversation, too, is personified, and readers are presented with the prospect of a *logos* (translated in the extract above as "discussion") that speaks back to its own inventors.

Finally, the adverb *teleōs* 'completely' again functions here on several interrelated levels of description at once. In this context, the adverb of completeness and fulfillment may be understood in terms of the argument under discussion, to which Socrates wishes to do justice. Metaphorically, it describes the payment of a conversational debt; but this financial sense is hardly a stretch, given that a major meaning of the verb *teleō* is 'to pay what one owes' (LSJ). Similarly, in both the semantic paradigm of its etymology and the syntax of the text, the adverb's proximity to the verb *teleutaō* suggests that an end, a *telos*, is near. Metatextually, this recognizes the ending of this long book as well, and all of these currents that meet in the adverb call attention to the texture itself. By drawing attention to its telling, the embedded tale of Er does not in any straightforward way simply advance a Platonic defense of justice. By prolonging the rewards of justice into the afterlife, the text proceeds, in both form and content, to trace a series of turns (rhetorical tropes that describe, for instance, the convolutions of Er's journey). It also stretches out the sense of an ending, suspending the book's *telos* indefinitely.

Er's Detour

The narrative structure of Socrates' tale of Er involves several major articulations. Socrates narrates how (on the previous day, in conversation) he reported the tale that was once told by a man named Er. Socrates calls Er a "messenger" (*angelon*, 619b), because this is what the judges in the afterlife call him: "They [the judges] said that he [Er] had to become a messenger to human beings of the things there, and they told him to listen and to look at everything in the place" (ἑαυτοῦ δὲ προσελθόντος εἰπεῖν ὅτι δέοι αὐτὸν <u>ἄγγελον</u> ἀνθρώποις γενέσθαι τῶν ἐκεῖ καὶ διακελεύοιντό οἱ ἀκούειν τε καὶ θεᾶσθαι πάντα τὰ ἐν τῷ τόπῳ, 614d). Thus Socrates reports that Er reports on judges' telling him to report back to mortals. And so when Er does report on his near-death experience, his tale in turn includes other speakers from whom he has heard about death and the beyond. Er hears and sees many things; among the speakers whose words are reported by Socrates, we have the following: the aforementioned judges who tell Er that he must become a messenger (614d); an unnamed individual who is overheard responding to another's question (Socrates is telling us that Socrates said, "now Er said that the man who was asked responded ... ," ἔφη οὖν τὸν ἐρωτώμενον εἰπεῖν, 615c–d); and there is a spokesman (*prophētēs*) who reports the *logos* of Lachesis (617d). The proliferation of voices is pronounced.

Because the judges do not let Er take a thousand-year journey, his report is based on overheard conversations: "The souls that were ever arriving looked as though they had come from a long *journey*.... And they *conversed* with one another" (καὶ τὰς ἀεὶ ἀφικνουμένας ὥσπερ ἐκ πολλῆς πορείας φαίνεσθαι ἥκειν ... διηγεῖσθαι δὲ ἀλλήλαις, 614e). Er's report is only possible at all because he takes a shortcut, making a detour from the usual long journey of death. The remoteness conveyed by the elaborate array of hearsay that constitutes his short tour, a journey through speakers who are speaking for other speakers (just as a *prophētēs* is one who speaks [*phēmi*] for [*pro-*] another), correlates to the remoteness of death itself, an ultimate and elusive object of knowledge, certain to be reached by all living souls yet known by none of them. For indeed, even Er himself does not go through the journey that dead souls take—he too can report only hearsay when it comes to the final journey. The cascade of reportage has the rhetorical effect of receding from the destination of ultimate truth like an echo from an unknown source. On the one hand, Er's evasion of the long journey is what allows his tale to be saved; on the other, the long trail of discourse recounted by Socrates is a substitute, a shortcut that is at a series of significant removes from the original destination.

While the journey traveled by dead souls after judgment is said to last a thousand years, this temporal distance is measured out by circular paths in space, by which souls go either up or down and then come back around (614c–d). These paths of judgment that lead above or below the earth resemble two other circular structures described in the tale: a spectacular image of the universe made of revolving, concentrically nested whorls (616b–617c), and the "death-bringing cycle" whose beginning (*arkhē*) is announced to dead souls when they are about to choose new lives and become mortal once again (617d–e). All of these are images of endlessness, conveying a sense of infinite recurrence in which ends turn back into beginnings. The complex circular movements of the universe offer a cosmic counterpoint to the paths of individual lives, and the sublime image of circles within circles evokes an unending sense of eternal recursion.[33] The cyclical movement through death and life is also concentric, in that the long journey after judgment is embedded, during death, inside the larger cycle of reincarnation. All in all, the paths in and of Socrates' narrative trace the journey of the soul with recurring circularity.

A New Beginning

Plato's text concludes with a long, complex sentence in which Socrates draws inspiration from the tale he has just retold.

> καὶ οὕτως, ὦ Γλαύκων, μῦθος ἐσώθη καὶ οὐκ ἀπώλετο, καὶ ἡμᾶς ἂν σώσειεν, ἂν πειθώμεθα αὐτῷ, καὶ τὸν τῆς Λήθης ποταμὸν εὖ διαβησόμεθα καὶ τὴν ψυχὴν οὐ μιανθησόμεθα. ἀλλ' ἂν ἐμοὶ πειθώμεθα, νομίζοντες ἀθάνατον ψυχὴν καὶ δυνατὴν πάντα μὲν κακὰ ἀνέχεσθαι, πάντα δὲ ἀγαθά, τῆς <u>ἄνω ὁδοῦ</u> ἀεὶ <u>ἑξόμεθα</u> καὶ δικαιοσύνην μετὰ φρονήσεως παντὶ <u>τρόπῳ</u> ἐπιτηδεύσομεν, ἵνα καὶ ἡμῖν αὐτοῖς φίλοι ὦμεν καὶ τοῖς θεοῖς, αὐτοῦ τε μένοντες ἐνθάδε, καὶ ἐπειδὰν τὰ ἆθλα αὐτῆς κομιζώμεθα, ὥσπερ οἱ νικηφόροι περιαγειρόμενοι, καὶ ἐνθάδε καὶ ἐν τῇ χιλιέτει <u>πορείᾳ</u>, ἣν <u>διεληλύθαμεν</u>, εὖ <u>πράττωμεν</u>.

> "And thus, Glaucon, a tale was saved and not lost; and it might save us, if we be persuaded by it, and we will make a good crossing of the river of Lethe and not defile our soul; but if we be persuaded by me, believing that soul is immortal and capable of bearing all evils and all goods, we will always hold [*hexometha*] to the upward path [*anō hodou*] and practice justice with prudence in every way [*tropōi*] so that we will be dear to ourselves and the gods, both while we remain here and when we reap the rewards for it like the victors who go about gathering in the prizes; and so here and in the thousand-year journey [*poreiai*] that we have gone through [*dielēluthamen*] we will fare [*prattōmen*] well … "

621b–d

Socrates' call is not so much a conclusion to the *Republic* as a transition from the tale of death to a new way of life. The text began midway through Socrates' homeward journey and it ends at yet another starting point. The main point of my analysis is that, while this sentence conveys a satisfying sense of closure by

---

[33] Where Bloom's translation has "bowls," the word *kados* 'jar, urn, box' gives us whorls like "boxes that fit into one another" (616d) in Shorey 1937, an image that happens to accord nicely with popular modern models of recursion such as Russian nesting dolls and Chinese boxes.

virtue of being a rousing (and rhetorically persuasive) exhortation, it also leads hopefully forward into an uncertain future. Although to my knowledge none has done so, it would not be inappropriate for a modern editor of the Greek text to end this breathless sentence with an ellipsis (and I have modified Bloom's translation with a final ellipsis to reflect this view). The sentence is neither a static confirmation of concluded arguments nor a narrative description of the conversation's end—the speaker here is Socrates the character, not Socrates the narrator. The speech's verve comes from a conditional, future-oriented, and dynamic emphasis on ongoing travel. Socrates is speculating about a journey of speculation, and rather than holding on to a fixed opinion, he hopes "we will always hold to the upward road," in an ongoing journey grounded in possibilities.

After a statement confirming that the tale, like Er himself, has survived death, the rest of the sentence concerns the afterlife of the tale. Grammatically, the remainder of Socrates' visionary prediction depends on two conditional clauses: "if we be persuaded by it" and "but if we be persuaded by me." These are difficult conditions to fulfill, since the tale of Er is a tall one, and it will surely be difficult to keep one's soul on an upward path. The appeal to different persuasive authorities, shifting from the tale to Socrates, pointedly distinguishes between "we" and "me" and thus maintains a distance between Socrates' present optimism and future deeds. Although Socrates here seems unusually and personally committed to something he is saying, the attitude expressed by his words is nevertheless far from certainty. He is making a noble prediction, relying heavily on the power of uplifting imagery and visionary sentiment as well as the appeal of future returns.

What Socrates is referring to by the "upward path" here is both mysterious and profoundly overdetermined. It could be an allusion to Hesiod's upward path of virtue, which is mentioned early in the *Republic*, at 364c–d).[34] In this immediate context, the path anticipates the thousand-year journey mentioned later in the sentence, while recalling the description of that journey given in Socrates' report of Er's report of what he heard and saw. As mapped out by the tale, the souls of Socrates and his listeners would themselves travel on an upward path, if they could live well enough to merit a good judgment when they died. The upward path (*anō hodon*) here may also be associated with the "path above" (*epanō hodon*, 514b) in the Cave; and the philosopher's ascent from the cave (*anabainō* + *anō*, 517a; *anō anabasin* and *anodon*, 517b); and the paths (*hodoi*) of dialectic (532d–e) that are prefigured by cognitive paths seen in the Divided Line (509d–511e).[35] By recalling all these paths when predicting the soul's

---

[34] See Halliwell 1988, at 621c5, with note to 619e2–5.
[35] See Schur 1998:73–82.

continuing journey on the paths of death and life, Socrates' words embed the methodological preoccupations of his conversation into a vision of sublimely recursive travel.

With one last occurrence of the verb *dierkhomai* 'to go through', the thousand-year journey described in the discourse of Er is said to have been described in the larger discourse of the conversation whose length has been self-consciously noted throughout the *Republic*.[36] The Greek phrase *eu prattō* simply means 'to do well' and 'farewell'. Yet the very last word of Plato's text is also a verb that stresses ongoing practice and travel. In its literal and etymological senses, *prattō* 'to do, fare' is an impeccable synonym for *dierkhomai*, inviting a comparison between paths of discourse and of method. And *prattō* is aptly translated by the English word *fare* because both words, like *dierkhomai*, are anchored in the semantic idea of 'passing through'.[37] Thus the ongoing methodical practice envisioned in Socrates' final words may be said to include further speculative conversation, more going through ideas in words.

---

[36] Jowett and Campbell see "a playful suggestion of our having made the pilgrimage ourselves" (1894, *ad loc.*). Adam, however, does not concur with them (1902, *ad loc.*). From a literary perspective, the suggestion can hardly be ignored.

[37] In Homer *prattō* occurs (as *prēssō*) with the meaning 'to traverse, to accomplish (a journey)' (LSJ). Etymologically, English *fare* and Greek *poros* 'way, passage' derive ultimately from the same root, meaning 'to pass through' (see OED; and Chantraine 2009, s.v. *peirō*). Cf. *aporia* and *wayfarer*.

5

Digressing toward a Possible Regime

ALTHOUGH THE BASIC TRAJECTORY of the *Republic* could certainly be understood in other ways, one can see the conversation rising from the Piraeus (in the wake of a spectacular event), moving through ideal political regimes and ascending to a high point of theoretical discussion in the middle, and then returning back down through degenerate regimes toward a vision of the afterlife. The conversation gradually becomes a self-conscious investigation of justice, and then it reaches a zenith when Socrates identifies the Good as the highest object of knowledge. Socrates proclaims the knowledge of this ideal to be a precondition of philosophical engagement in political planning and ruling; and indeed, such knowledge is imagined as an educational precondition of philosophy itself.

But if the Good is introduced in the conversation as a profound ideal that should be pursued in education, so that it may be said to guide the ideal ruler of the ideal city-state, Socrates passes up the opportunity to account for the Good directly. As at other moments in the conversation, Socrates is here reluctant to keep talking about something difficult to address, but when it comes to the Good, he defers discussion of it indefinitely. By talking about the sun instead of the Good, Socrates takes a detour from which the conversation will never return. On the one hand, this conversation designed by Plato is an illuminating discussion of profound topics, and whatever else the text may do, it does shed light on these difficult and elusive issues. On the other hand, where we might expect the conversation to reach certain conclusions, it features talk *about* reaching them instead. In this sense, the book reaches a methodological nadir at its approximate center: it describes method as approximation. It may seem churlish to complain about the missing Good when Socrates gives us so much to think about, but within the framework of conversation led by Socrates, the Good is not just emphatically avoided but also crucially important. And while it is obvious that the Good is missing from the conversation, this chapter and the next do not critique the argument so much as consider examples of *how* evasive methodological rhetoric functions in the text. This chapter focuses on the development of an ideal regime, and the next one considers the place of the Good in the sequence of Sun, Divided Line, and Cave.

Questions of Procedure

In Book 2, after listening to arguments by Glaucon and Adeimantus, who have been extolling injustice for the sake of argument, Socrates agrees to defend justice on the condition that the conversation adopt a particular methodical approach: to look for justice (and injustice) in the city-state, where its greater magnitude will make it easier to see than in the individual (368b–369b). My concern here is not whether an equivalence between justice in the individual and in the state is a logically valid premise. Let us note instead that it is a premise whose function belongs to a fundamental trend in the discussion overall: nonasserted arguments are entertained *for the sake of furthering the discussion*, particularly in order to overcome difficulties. Hypotheses or suppositions for which no one claims any certainty are frequently accepted as grounds for extensive discussion. Elaborate theories are thus built on foundations acknowledged as uncertain and accepted only conditionally. The conversation in the *Republic* regularly relies on conventions of rational agreement—the conversation is not an aimless free-for-all—but while doing so it thrives on claims that are permeated by disclaimers. In the *Republic*, heuristic conversation tends to move forward by turning aside.

Right before Socrates suggests that they design a city-state, both Glaucon and Adeimantus have been playing devil's advocate and recommending injustice; Glaucon even goes so far as to remind Socrates, "don't suppose that it is I who speak" (μὴ ἐμὲ οἴου λέγειν, 361e). Attributing one's own utterances to others and pretending to adopt their views is a common rhetorical structure in the *Republic*, a simple way to speak without endorsing what one is saying.[1] Quotations from traditional writers are a variation of the same gesture. Localized instances of this trope in the *Republic* are embedded in a larger structure of the same type: Socrates reports the speech of others (including a mediated version of himself) when he narrates the previous day's conversation. And Socrates the narrator is embedded in Plato's text. Narrating in the first person, Socrates is named by others as a character in the narrative, while his narrating voice is mediated by constraints of ahistoricity and fictionality, given that the historical Socrates was dead when Plato wrote. Every speaker named in the text is participating in a discussion under someone else's name, with the author retreating to exaggerated distances from the utterances of his imagined speakers.

---

[1] See Blondell 2002:190–199, and also her observation on "ventriloquations" (42).

But if Plato is a structurally and rhetorically distant source or origin of what is reported in Socrates' narrative as having been said by speakers in Socrates' narrative, the narrative introduces a comparable distance in the form of a gap between the seekers and their goals. When Socrates proposes his innovation in method to his fellow talkers, he first remarks that their powers of sight are inadequate to the task of seeking something like justice, something that is both very abstract and very important. (I presume that Socrates is here acknowledging a widespread weakness of human cognition generally.)

In the passage that shifts attention from individual to city-state (368b-369b), Socrates explicitly, and tentatively, establishes a methodological version of heuristic conversation. It is a procedure of "seeking" (*zētēsis*, 368d) a "sought object" (*zētēma*, 368c), fundamentally visual in its conceptual vocabulary, and hinging on a possible "resemblance" (*homoiotēs*, 369a) between the city-state and the individual.[2] Socrates introduces this method of comparison by making a hypothetical comparison: looking for justice in the city (which might be like the individual) might be like reading a text with big print. The comparison with reading is further complicated because it contains an imaginary scenario, a hypothetical (and in this instance contrafactual) condition: "If someone had ordered men who don't see very sharply to read little letters from a distance [*porrōthen*]," the readers would gladly start by reading a larger version of the same letters—"*if* they happen to be the same" (εἰ προσέταξέ τις γράμματα σμικρὰ πόρρωθεν ἀναγνῶναι μὴ πάνυ ὀξὺ βλέπουσιν ... εἰ τὰ αὐτὰ ὄντα τυγχάνει, 368d). Although perhaps not unusual for Plato's Socrates, the verbal convolutions here are otherwise extraordinary: justice in the individual is nested in the city-state like a subset in a set; the likeness between city-state and individual is nested in a likeness between seeking and reading, which in turn derives (rhetorically) from an imaginary, conditional situation; and the hypothetical situation is a theoretical, metavisual, and metatextual image of perspectival distance in the process of reading. We are reading about readers reading, and we are speculating about methods of speculation by looking at images of looking, using a possible resemblance in order to entertain a possible method of looking.

Even Socrates' proposal in response to the inadequacy of sight is a retrospective, corrective disclaimer: the best procedure for seeking justice and injustice may be different from what he and the others have been following. This disclaimer is itself qualified; Socrates uses qualifying expressions such as "it appears [*phainetai*] to me" and "it seems to me [*dokō*]" (368d); "perhaps" (*isōs*)

---

2   So, as recalled at 430d, the entire investigation (verb = *zēteō*) is for the sake of finding justice (*dikaiosunē*) in itself. And this investigation may be said to fit within the defense of the benefits of justice that replaces the initial attempt to define justice as a kind of behavior.

and "if you wish" (368e); and hortatory verb forms of invitation: "let us seek" (*zētēsōmen*) and then "let us examine" (*episkepsōmetha*) at 369a.

In looking at the methodological exchange between Socrates and Adeimantus, we may also revisit a future-less-vivid condition touched on in chapter 3. A question of procedure, based on a conditional premise, becomes a chain of theoretical argument:

ἆρ' οὖν, ἦν δ' ἐγώ, εἰ γιγνομένην πόλιν θεασαίμεθα λόγῳ, καὶ τὴν δικαιοσύνην αὐτῆς ἴδοιμεν ἂν γιγνομένην καὶ τὴν ἀδικίαν;

τάχ' ἄν, ἦ δ' ὅς.

οὐκοῦν γενομένου αὐτοῦ ἐλπὶς εὐπετέστερον ἰδεῖν ὃ ζητοῦμεν;

πολύ γε.

"If we should watch [*theasaimetha*] a city-state coming into being in discourse," I said, "would we also see [*idoimen*] its justice coming into being, and its injustice?"

"Probably," he said.

"When this has been done, there is hope [*elpis*] of seeing [*idein*] what we're seeking [*zētoumen*] more easily?"

"Far more easily."

369a–b

Here the hope held out by the second question depends on our accepting the conditional statement (if we should watch that, we would see this) posed in the first question. The second question functions much like the first: if we see that, then there is hope of seeing this. The argument confirms the theoretical (intellectually visual) underpinnings of the proposed approach, and we may recall that the modern notion of *theory* derives from the Greek verb *theaomai* 'to watch'. Socrates' appeal to ease may also be read as a gesture of compromise. Here we may compare a saying quoted by Glaucon later in the dialogue during a consideration of method and path: "The fine things are difficult [*khalepa*]."[3] This crucial step in the conversation remains open to doubt and may also be a shortcut, capitulating to the difficulty of investigating this important topic.

---

[3]   At 435c; cf. 328e, 364d, 435d, 497d, 498a, 499d, 504b; and see Schur 1998:60–65.

The Short Path to a Definition

Perhaps the most prominent and sustained focus of the conversation recounted by Socrates is the topic of justice, which in turn leads to that of political organization, which leads to education, which can result in a philosopher-ruler, on whom the possibility of a just *politeia* would depend. Justice thus serves as both a starting point and a goal. As a quality achieved at the pinnacle of philosophical education, justice is a goal. At the same time, neither a just *politeia* nor an adequate educational curriculum can rightly be developed without first understanding justice, and that will require an understanding of the Good. The conversation makes repeated attempts to design a just regime for a city-state. The first try is compared to a city of pigs (372d), and the second plan, later complemented by a description of degenerate regimes, gives way to the need for radical social and educational changes.

A definition of justice is nevertheless reached in Book 4 (443b–444a), and this definition seems generally to be accepted by scholars as a solid achievement and a proposition asserted by Plato in the *Republic*. Before moving through some passages concerning the planning of an ideal city-state, let us take a closer look at how Socrates articulates the definition. After looking for four virtues in the city-state and finally finding a version of justice there, Socrates hesitates to claim victory until, in accordance with the method of reading large letters, justice has also been found in the individual.[4] Before this can be done, Socrates yet again halts for a major methodological concern, because the conversation must determine whether the human soul is indeed structured like a city-state (434d–435d). Glaucon agrees about the seriousness of this problem, and this is when he notes that "fine things are difficult [*khalepa*]" (χαλεπὰ τὰ καλά, 435c). Socrates wonders whether they should take a shortcut:

> ὡς ἡ ἐμὴ δόξα, ἀκριβῶς μὲν τοῦτο ἐκ τοιούτων <u>μεθόδων</u>, οἵαις νῦν ἐν τοῖς <u>λόγοις</u> χρώμεθα, οὐ μή ποτε λάβωμεν—ἄλλη γὰρ <u>μακροτέρα</u> καὶ πλείων <u>ὁδὸς</u> ἡ ἐπὶ τοῦτο <u>ἄγουσα</u> —ἴσως μέντοι τῶν γε προειρημένων τε καὶ προεσκεμμένων ἀξίως.

> "In my opinion, we'll never get a precise grasp of it on the basis of procedures [*methodōn*] such as we're now using in the argument [*logos*]. There is another longer [*makrotera*] and further road [*hodos*] leading

---

4   At 434d. See Cross and Woozley 1964: "Despite the fact that the order of exposition is first city and then individual, Plato's order of argument is the other way round, from individual to city" (111).

[*agousa*] to it. But perhaps we can do it in a way worthy of what's been said and considered before."

435c–d

By taking this shortcut, the speakers clearly make a compromise, and Socrates will later refer back to this decision (504b, 504c; discussed below). The detour here is a turn away from the longer path, and the shorter path of method is preferred because it is easier; it keeps the conversation going, but it is another deviation from the best path.

Although there is agreement in the conversation regarding the resulting definition of justice (which describes justice as a harmonious disposition of the soul), Socrates consistently qualifies his commitment to it, and he sums up his attitude in a peculiar exchange with Glaucon:

εἶεν, ἦν δ' ἐγώ: τὸν μὲν δίκαιον καὶ ἄνδρα καὶ πόλιν καὶ δικαιοσύνην, ὃ τυγχάνει ἐν αὐτοῖς ὄν, εἰ <u>φαῖμεν ηὑρηκέναι</u>, οὐκ ἂν πάνυ τι οἶμαι <u>δόξαιμεν</u> ψεύδεσθαι.

μὰ Δία οὐ μέντοι, ἔφη.

<u>φῶμεν</u> ἄρα;

<u>φῶμεν</u>.

"All right," I said. "If we should assert [*phaimen*] that we have found [*hēurēkenai*] the just man and city and what justice really is in them, I don't suppose we would seem [*doxaimen*] to be telling an utter lie."

"By Zeus, no indeed," he said.

"Let's assert [*phōmen*] it then?"

"Let's assert it."

444a

Instead of declaring that justice has been found, Socrates makes a hyperbolically indirect and metaconversational observation that functions as a question. He begins with a future-less-vivid condition about making an assertion. The second half of the conditional statement (the then-clause) is a negative conjecture ("I don't suppose") about possibly seeming to say something exaggeratedly wrong. On the basis of this fantastically noncommittal utterance, Socrates and Glaucon agree, using hortatory subjunctives ("let us assert"), to assert something. But that is the extent of their eureka moment: instead of asserting—they talk *about* asserting it. With a third-person imperative—"so be it"—Socrates is ready to move on, even though he is also about to embark on his greatest detour.

Socrates' Great Detour

Before Socrates can deliver a description of philosophy (which leads into a discussion of philosopher-rulers, their qualifications, and their education), he is repeatedly pressed to say whether the imaginary *politeia* 'political organiza-tion' of Callipolis could ever be realized in practice. For many interpreters of the *Republic*, Plato's own opinion on this question has been an especially conten-tious issue.[5] This section of the current study focuses instead on the rhetor-ical expression of possibility in a series of subordinated conditions. Socrates develops his response by referring to the philosophical role of *logos* 'discourse, thought', of rational thought conceived in language, and his proposed resolu-tion appeals to the notion of a *paradeigma* 'model, pattern', an ideal that the philosophically minded may strive to approximate and imitate. This open-ended proposal comes after a series of diversionary tactics, which are them-selves noted and discussed in the conversation. In yet another self-consciously adopted methodological evasion, the *politeia* is envisioned as a model. And a self-reflective idealization of the conversation's own efforts emerges.

When Socrates finally addresses the problem of possibility at length, he makes a methodological point about the difference between word and deed, asking his companions to accept that their *politeia* should be understood as a *paradeigma* 'model, pattern' that does not even need to be feasible in practice (471a–473a, 592a–b). And the account of the *politeia* is a kind of thematic state-ment (not asserted by the author), made by speakers (characters) who them-selves expressly back away from asserting its reality. *Socrates invokes the model as an explicitly evasive maneuver.*

The investigation of justice undertaken by these characters, as portrayed in Socrates' account of the model's usefulness, is thus far removed from its goal. A model, in the accounts at 471a–473a in Book 5 and at 592a–b in Book 9, is clearly not an *eidos* 'Form'; instead of being a perfect, immortal, unchanging, and single Reality, a model such as the *politeia* is made by human beings. Yet it is certainly something akin to an *eidos*, and in other passages of the book, it appears to have much the same function.[6] We could attribute Socrates' variable use of the term to Plato's penchant for turning casual words into his technical vocabulary, but

---

[5] So Annas 1981:185.
[6] See *Republic* 500d and Fujisawa 1974.

one of the main implications of the present chapter is that the whole idea of a
distinctly technical vocabulary of Platonic philosophy becomes untenable when
the verbal texture in which arguments (about Forms, for instance) appear is
taken into account. When a thematic term such as *eidos* recurs in casual (but
methodical) conversation, its technical status is modalized, while the conversation's focus on itself continually feeds attention to method as an endless
pursuit. At the same time, the context in which the *politeia* is called a model is,
if not technical, momentous, because a pronouncement on the feasibility of the
politeia is repeatedly broached and delayed (450c, 466d), and the postponement
is itself explicitly noted (458a, 471c).[7]

At the beginning of Book 5, Socrates is once again pushed by the others
to elaborate on difficult topics when he sees himself reaching a conclusion of
sorts.[8] In particular, Adeimantus and the others want more details about the
treatment of women and children in the political state that the conversationalists have been imagining, and this is a thorny topic in part because of its radical
departure from Greek cultural conventions. Under considerable teasing pressure, Socrates protests:

οἷον, ἦν δ' ἐγώ, εἰργάσασθε ἐπιλαβόμενοί μου. ὅσον <u>λόγον</u> πάλιν,
ὥσπερ ἐξ ἀρχῆς, <u>κινεῖτε</u> περὶ τῆς πολιτείας· ἣν ὡς ἤδη <u>διεληλυθὼς</u> ἐγώ
γε ἔχαιρον, ἀγαπῶν εἴ τις ἐάσοι ταῦτα ἀποδεξάμενος ὡς τότε ἐρρήθη. ἃ
νῦν ὑμεῖς παρακαλοῦντες.

> "Think of how much discussion [*logon*] about the state you are setting
> in motion [*kineite*] again as if we were starting from the beginning. And
> to think how pleased I was myself at how much we had already gone
> through [*dielēluthōs*] and delighted if anyone accepted what was said at
> that point and allowed it to stand."

450a–b

I draw attention to the verbs *kineō* 'to set in motion' and *dierkhomai* 'to go
through', which characterize the conversation as a dynamic movement that
is being forced to continue. The word *dierkhomai* (which can also mean 'to
pass through, complete') is often used (in a perfectly ordinary manner) in the

---

[7]   The feasibility of realizing the *politeia* in actual circumstances is an important part of the third
and most intimidating wave of paradox that ushers in the philosopher as an ideal ruler (472a).
"Seldom does Plato build his reader's anticipations so deliberately" (Pappas 2013:137).

[8]   Like other commentators, Shorey 1937 views Books 5 through 7 as a digression, but adds,
"'Digression' need not imply that these books were not a part of the original design" (*ad loc.*). So
Emlyn-Jones and Preddy: "Structurally a long digression, Books 5–7 actually contain the philo-
sophical core of *Republic*" (2013, *ad loc.*). See also Goldschmidt 1963:136.

Republic to describe the movement of the discussion, the participants having traveled through topics by means of words.

At the prospect of going back to a beginning, Socrates worries that the discussion may get too long, but Glaucon gushes that thoughtful people would be willing to spend their whole lives listening to such a discussion (450b). Even though Glaucon is telling him to proceed without worrying, Socrates remains apprehensive:

> οὐ ῥᾴδιον, ὦ εὔδαιμον, ἦν δ᾽ ἐγώ, <u>διελθεῖν</u>: πολλὰς γὰρ <u>ἀπιστίας</u> ἔχει ἔτι μᾶλλον τῶν ἔμπροσθεν ὧν <u>διήλθομεν</u>. καὶ γὰρ ὡς δυνατὰ λέγεται, <u>ἀπιστοῖτ᾽</u> ἄν, καὶ εἰ ὅτι μάλιστα γένοιτο, ὡς ἄριστ᾽ ἂν εἴη ταῦτα, καὶ ταύτῃ <u>ἀπιστήσεται</u>. διὸ δὴ καὶ ὄκνος τις αὐτῶν ἅπτεσθαι, μὴ εὐχὴ <u>δοκῇ</u> εἶναι ὁ <u>λόγος</u>, ὦ φίλε ἑταῖρε.

> "It isn't easy to go through [*dielthein*], my dear fellow," I said. "It admits of many doubts: even more than the matters we went through [*diēlthomen*] before. For one might doubt [*apistoite*] the things we are proposing are possible, and even if they were actually to turn out to be so, even here there might be doubt [*apistēsetai*] as to whether they would be for the best. For this reason I feel a certain reluctance to touch on these matters in case the discourse [*logos*] might seem [*dokēi*] like wishful thinking, my friend."

450c–d

Here we can observe complicated elements of qualification in Socrates' hesitation, when the difficulty of explaining difficulties is aggravated by doubt. Socrates has not just a quantity of separate doubts but an accumulation of doubts in which some are subordinated to others. "It isn't easy to go through" here presumably conveys the (metaconversational) difficulty of explaining the controversial conditions for women, children, and guardians in the *politeia*; but these are also doubts about continuing the conversation and about explaining the doubts. The second occurrence of *dierkhomai*, in the phrase "matters we went through before," evidently refers to the subject matter of the discussion, casting doubt on earlier stages of the conversation and thus calling the discussion's cumulative chain of argumentation into question. The two uses of the same verb in close proximity give a microcosmic view of the dialogue's self-reflective preoccupation with method; the idea of verbal movement draws a parallel between the verbal articulation of current metaconversational difficulties and an earlier part of the conversation into which these difficulties are being projected back, rhetorically, and in which they are embedded. This digressive pause in the conversation is in fact no less a part of the overall conversation (or of the overall design of the *Republic*) for being self-reflective.

The ensuing series of doubts, which Socrates raises impersonally, as though they might be raised by an unidentified doubter, is perhaps an even more characteristic example of Socratic rhetoric (in the *Republic*, at least). Far from directly addressing reality himself, Socrates wonders whether someone else might potentially doubt whether these newer proposals for the imagined *politeia* would be possible. This possible doubting of possibility is then the condition for the potential question as to whether the innovations would be beneficial. And finally, as a result of these imaginable doubtings, Socrates wonders whether the discussion itself could end up so far from reality that no one would take it seriously. In this stacking of conditional statements, subsequent conditions are rhetorically subordinated to previous ones, with modal verb forms (optatives and a subjunctive) at each step taking the discourse even further from certitude.

Undaunted by this cascade of doubt, Glaucon tells Socrates not to hesitate, because his listeners are ready and willing to hear more. But this only makes Socrates more anxious, sending him into a lengthy explanation of his self-doubt; he says he is comfortable speaking "when I believe [*pisteuontos*] myself that I know what I am talking about [*ha legō*]" (πιστεύοντος μὲν γὰρ ἐμοῦ ἐμοὶ εἰδέναι ἃ λέγω, 450d). But when he is "doubting [*apistounta*], and at the same time seeking [*zētounta*] to express myself [*logous poieisthai*]" (ἀπιστοῦντα δὲ καὶ ζητοῦντα ἅμα τοὺς λόγους ποιεῖσθαι, 450e), like right now, he runs into trouble. Socrates here uses the same verb (*apisteō* 'to disbelieve, distrust, doubt') that he used above when describing the hypothetical doubts that someone might have regarding their conversation. Those doubts have now joined his own, and he is threatening to bring the conversation to a standstill—but instead of bringing conclusive completeness, the standstill is a pileup of uncertainty, to the point where Socrates is now reflecting generally about his uncertainties rather than about this specific conversation, let alone the *politeia*.

By claiming to be extremely unsure of himself as a knower and a speaker, Socrates does not disavow knowledge so much as make no claims to it. And Socrates' disclaimers not only concern knowledge in itself—knowledge about good policies for an ideal state; they also distance him from knowledge about his own knowledge (knowledge of himself) and from the knowledge needed for proper verbal expression. The Greek expression *ha legō* clearly denotes "what I am talking about," referring to the subject matter for discussion, but Socrates' search for the right words (*logoi*) reinforces the more literal sense: "what I am saying." Either way, Socrates' own words put reflexive emphasis on the difficulty of finding the right language for investigation and explanation. Indeed, the verb *zēteō* 'to seek' is here turned away from the supposed goals of the investigation and back toward the use of language, suggesting how involute the procedure of investigation can become in its self-reflection.

Before allowing himself to be pressed into explaining the treatment of women and children in the *politeia*, and the education of the state's guardians, Socrates describes a feared situation in which

ἀλλὰ μὴ σφαλεὶς τῆς ἀληθείας οὐ μόνον αὐτὸς ἀλλὰ καὶ τοὺς φίλους συνεπισπασάμενος κείσομαι περὶ ἃ ἥκιστα δεῖ σφάλλεσθαι.

"not only tripping up regarding the truth myself, I will lie prostrate, having also dragged my friends with me concerning things about which one ought least to trip up."

451a

Whether this dramatic picture of Socrates and friends tumbling into error is tragic, comic, or both, one might compare it with the scenario of the cave as a descent toward death and murder, because Socrates rounds out this volley of doubts by declaring he would rather commit involuntary manslaughter than mislead his friends in a discussion of important topics. Be that as it may, the imagery of tripping, lying down, and dragging participates in a network of metaphors frequently used in Plato, in Greek, and in general to describe methodical movement. The prospect of tripping and falling in the pursuit of truth, viewed as murder of a sort, is a rhetorically forceful articulation of the speaker's hesitation to continue speaking. Glaucon laughingly reassures Socrates that the others will not hold him responsible for any investigative crimes occasioned by the *logos* 'discourse, thought' (451b). And so this digression concerning doubts and fears, which is described by the narrator as a moment in the conversation where a near ending got turned into a new beginning, functions to qualify the discourse concerning women, children, and education that follows, which is itself a digression from the topic of conversation that preceded.

Alas, Socrates' reluctance to take a stand on the *politeia*'s practicability (a problem that will hinge on the participation of a philosopher-ruler) continues unabated. In a subsequent moment of postponement, Socrates confesses he had hoped to "run away" (*apodidraskō*) from the problem of feasibility by focusing on whether the *politeia* would be beneficial. When Glaucon says, "you have not been running away [*apodidraskōn*] unnoticed" (ἀλλ᾽ οὐκ ἔλαθες, ἦ δ᾽ ὅς, ἀποδιδράσκων, 457e), Socrates asks for a reprieve: "But just grant me this much: allow me to take a holiday [*heortasai*], just as lazy people like to make a feast of their thoughts when they are traveling [*poreuōntai*] alone" (τοσόνδε μέντοι χαρισαίμοι· ἔασόν με ἑορτάσαι, ὥσπερ οἱ ἀργοὶ τὴν διάνοιαν εἰώθασιν ἑστιᾶσθαι ὑφ᾽ ἑαυτῶν, ὅταν μόνοι <u>πορεύωνται</u>, 457e–458a). In the figurative, metaconversational vocabulary of the conversation, running away has been one of two concurrent flight tactics; the other has been "to flee through" (*diapheugō*, 457b; see also 472a) difficult topics, as through increasingly big waves.[9]

Socrates now proceeds to put a self-deprecating but more positive spin on the notion of escape, while the third wave (the need for rulers to be trained in philosophy) is still encroaching, carrying with it the issue of practicability. Socrates asks to be indulged like a lazy daydreamer, using the verb *poreuō* 'to walk, travel' in a physical sense, which we would ordinarily call literal, in order to create a generalizing image of daydreamers who wander around. This same image, of people literally wandering, is here part of a simile that depends on the metaphor of taking a holiday (*heortazō* 'to keep festival or holiday'), which gives the literal traveling a figurative turn.[10] The simile as a whole describes how Socrates would like to continue describing the *politeia* as though it were possible and "to postpone" (*anabalesthai*, 458b) an examination of feasibility. By incorporating an image of physical travel into a simile about conversational procedure (and thus rendering the literal figurative by putting it inside a figure), Socrates' language again shows us that a detour (an evasive maneuver introduced during a metaconversational aside) can allow the conversation to keep moving.

Dodging the *Politeia*

Having secured a reprieve (458b), Socrates continues traveling-conversing as though the group's plans for the *politeia*'s guardians could possibly be put into practice. Eventually, however, Glaucon fears that Socrates' detour will never end; he insists on returning to the topic of "the possibility of this *politeia* coming into being and how it could ever be done" (471c). Socrates says that Glaucon's unexpected "raid" (*katadromē*) on his "discourse" (*logos*) is bringing on the third wave of difficulty (472a). Whereas Socrates has been traveling freely, without having to worry about whether his theoretical discourse conforms to physical reality, Glaucon is making an incursion from the practical world. And in response, Socrates takes the significant methodological step of describing the imagined *politeia* as an idealized portrait.

To repeat, the question is, could the *politeia* actually exist? (Followed by the next question: Could a lover of wisdom ever rule an earthly state?) Socrates' answer is a profound dodge. On the one hand, he is now confronting rather than

---

[9]   The three waves of controversy concern the equality of male and female guardians, the disposition of women and children as common property, and the need for a philosopher-ruler (457c–d, 472a, 473c).

[10]   On festivals, feasting, travel, and theory, see Nightingale 2004:75–76.

evading the problem of feasibility. On the other hand, he asks that the investigation proceed in accordance with a policy of methodical evasion. If everybody would agree that the *politeia* does not need to be possible, then its possibility could be bracketed, in effect making the problem into a nonproblem. Just as Socrates wanted to wander earlier, now he would adopt a method of approximation. In my analysis, his call to approach the *politeia* as a model has recursive qualities, admitting the prospect that the unending, insuperable conceptual distance that accumulates from these stacked conditions might come between the conversational search and its envisioned goals.

Before explaining how a model like this might work, Socrates wishes to establish that the question of possibility is now on the table because the group has been engaged in a goal-oriented journey of seeking: "First it should be recalled that we arrived here [*deuro*] while seeking [*zētountes*] what justice and injustice are like" (πρῶτον μὲν τόδε χρὴ ἀναμνησθῆναι, ὅτι ἡμεῖς ζητοῦντες δικαιοσύνην οἷόν ἐστι καὶ ἀδικίαν δεῦρο ἥκομεν, 472b). Socrates then asks Glaucon to choose between two conditional statements:

ἀλλ' ἐὰν εὕρωμεν οἷόν ἐστι δικαιοσύνη, ἆρα καὶ ἄνδρα τὸν δίκαιον ἀξιώσομεν μηδὲν δεῖν αὐτῆς ἐκείνης διαφέρειν, ἀλλὰ πανταχῇ τοιοῦτον εἶναι οἷον δικαιοσύνη ἐστίν; ἢ ἀγαπήσομεν ἐὰν ὅτι ἐγγύτατα αὐτῆς ᾖ καὶ πλεῖστα τῶν ἄλλων ἐκείνης μετέχῃ;

"If we find [*heurōmen*] what justice is like, will we also insist that the just man must not differ at all from justice itself but in every way be such as it is? Or will we be content [*agapēsomen*] if he is nearest [*engutata*] to it and participates in it more than the others?"

472b–c

The choice depends, in the first place, on figuring out what justice is; Socrates now evidently does not think that this has been accomplished.[11] As we have seen, the definition was accepted earlier in very roundabout and questioning terms (444a), and now the status of that earlier conclusion has been downgraded, making the knowledge of justice only conditionally accessible, and far from accepted (as of this latest reflection on the conversation, at least). As a consequence, the verb *agapaō* 'to be pleased, content' acquires a sense of compromise when Glaucon says that he and his companions would be content with a practical reality that came close to the ideal (472c).

---

[11] Shorey 1937 *ad loc.* writes, "Plato seems to overlook the fact that the search was virtually completed in the fourth book."

Socrates thereupon submits that the investigation of justice has been "for the sake of a model [*paradeigmatos*]" (παραδείγματος ἄρα ἕνεκα, 472c). As he prepares to explain philosophy as the love and pursuit of wisdom (474b–480), Socrates here reconsiders what the conversation has been trying to do, allowing that the knowledge of justice-in-itself was not the final goal. If justice could possibly be found (and Socrates is no longer saying that it has been) in conversation, then its verbal portrait could (possibly) serve as a model for pursuing wisdom in everyday life, and thus wisdom could (possibly) be realized—as justice, for instance, in a city-state. Although Socrates denies the possibility neither of realizing justice in everyday life nor of making a perfect model of it in speech, finding the perfect model would be a condition for creating an imperfect earthly city-state, and a spirit of compromise is invading the entire project of the investigation.

Socrates gets a concession from Glaucon that is based on their earlier agreement: if justice could be found, the man nearest to that ideal would meet their criteria sufficiently enough to be deemed a candidate. Socrates asks for permission to forgo worrying about enacting what "we went through in discourse [*diēlthomen*]" (τῷ λόγῳ διήλθομεν, 473a):

> ἀλλ', ἐὰν οἷοί τε γενώμεθα εὑρεῖν ὡς ἂν ἐγγύτατα τῶν εἰρημένων πόλις οἰκήσειεν, φάναι ἡμᾶς ἐξηυρηκέναι ὡς δυνατὰ ταῦτα γίγνεσθαι ἃ σὺ ἐπιτάττεις. ἢ οὐκ ἀγαπήσεις τούτων τυγχάνων;

> "But if we are able to find [*heurein*] that a city-state could be governed in a way most nearly [*engutata*] approximating what has been said, say that we've found [*exēurēkenai*] the possibility of these things' coming into being on which you insist. Or won't you be content [*agapēseis*] if it turns out this way?"

> 473a–b

The methodological concession is again expressed in the form of a complex condition, with the attainment of one goal dependent on reaching another. If it should prove possible to find (*heuriskō*) that a government near enough to their verbal model was possible, then they would say that they had found (*heuriskō*) the possibility of realizing the city-state in deed. I take it that "what has been said" refers to a plan, a *paradeigma*, that would be like, but is no longer necessarily equivalent to, the definitions of a just man and a just *politeia* that were reached earlier in the conversation. In any case, Glaucon agrees that he would be content with Socrates' proposed preference for verbal portraiture over practical implementation. Having agreed already that "it is the nature of action to attain to less truth than does speaking" (φύσιν ἔχει πρᾶξιν λέξεως ἧττον ἀληθείας ἐφάπτεσθαι, 473a), Glaucon now allows, in effect, that if something could come close to an ideal verbal portrait, it would be close to the truth, regardless of actual reality.[12]

The verbal aspect of the *paradeigma* so described is expressed by the word *logos* (472e, 473a), while I refer to portraiture because both here (472d) and later (500d–501c) Socrates uses the example of a painter to explain the exemplary function of an ideal verbal model. Here Socrates points out that observers are not concerned about physical reality when a painter draws an idealized portrait of a human being, a *paradeigma* (472d). "Weren't we, as we assert, also making [*epoioumen*] a pattern [*paradeigma*] in discourse [*logoi*] of a good city?" asks Socrates (οὐ καὶ ἡμεῖς, φαμέν, <u>παράδειγμα ἐποιοῦμεν λόγῳ</u> ἀγαθῆς πόλεως; 472d–e). For those interpreters who see in Socrates' notion of a paradigm an anticipation of a more technical Form (*eidos*) to be introduced later, this comparison between conversing and painting puts the conversational investigation in an odd light. If the group has been seeking—hunting near and far—to find an abstract ideal of justice in order to see and understand its true nature, they have simultaneously been making (*poieō* 'to make, create') a portrait of the just city in words. If this is so, then their verbal pattern of a good city, contrary to our expectations, did not proceed from a prior understanding of justice. Indeed, they began to draw up the pattern of a political system in order to understand justice in the individual, and then they returned to the individual before accepting their account of justice in the city-state. Were they ready, we might wonder, to create an ideal pattern, which would in turn be worth contemplating from the imperfect perspective of Athenian citizens?[13] Or were they just practicing, getting a foretaste of philosophical inquiry by talking about how one might talk about abstract ideals? Perhaps they are being presented to us all as role models in the making?

These questions become more pointed when, a bit further on, we find Socrates describing the ideal philosopher-ruler as both an imitator of truths and a maker of models (500a–501c). This happens once Socrates has introduced the need for a philosopher-ruler, at a moment when he also becomes much

---

12 Reeve, who strongly discounts the idea that the *Republic* is "vitiated by equivocation" (1988:xii), takes the view that Plato is in fact outlining a third polis at 473b4–544b3 (170). Given the repeated displacement of one plan by another, it seems to me one must be sure that the planning has reached completion once and for all if it is to avoid retroactive vitiation (or modalization); Reeve finds each previous plan included and assimilated inside the next, and he stops at three (172). For Cross and Woozley 1964, "the third and final city is entirely different" from its predecessors, "in that it is based on a political principle," but this third city is more or less Reeve's second (99).

13 Benardete 1992 discerns two cities in the *Republic*, one made in speech by the group, the other being a dialogic city where Socrates is king and the others are spectators (46–47).

more sanguine about the possibility of philosophy's and politics' combining in practice (499b–c). And with the possibility of a philosopher-ruler seeming more imaginable, Socrates now even appears to revisit his doubts about the attainment of individual as well as political perfection (499b). As far as the current analysis is concerned, however, whether the possibility is deemed possible or not, the entire discussion continues to be modalized by evasive rhetorical expressions. When Socrates forcefully asserts that a philosopher might somehow come to rule, or that a ruler could develop "a true erotic passion for true philosophy," his statement takes a doubly negative form: "I deny that there is any reason why either or both of these things is impossible" (τούτων δὲ πότερα γενέσθαι ἢ ἀμφότερα ὡς ἄρα ἐστὶν ἀδύνατον, ἐγὼ μὲν οὐδένα φημὶ ἔχειν λόγον, 499c).

Socrates says more about city planning after he and Adeimantus have outlined some of the difficulties facing philosophy in everyday life, and concluded that there is currently no philosophical *politeia* in existence (497b). Understanding that they are back to discussing an envisioned, unrealized *politeia*, Adeimantus asks "whether it is the same one we have gone through [*dielēluthamen*] in founding the city-state" (εἰ αὐτὴ ἦν ἡμεῖς <u>διεληλύθαμεν</u> οἰκίζοντες τὴν πόλιν ἢ ἄλλη, 497c). After all, this very problem has guided much of the conversation thus far. Socrates' response is paradoxical. On the one hand, the *politeia* they are now talking about would be the same:

> δεήσοι <u>τι</u> ἀεὶ ἐνεῖναι ἐν τῇ πόλει λόγον ἔχον τῆς πολιτείας τὸν αὐτὸν ὅνπερ καὶ σὺ ὁ νομοθέτης ἔχων τοὺς νόμους ἐτίθεις.

> "There would always have to be present in the city something [*ti*] possessing the same understanding of the regime as you, the lawgiver, had when you were setting down the laws."

> 497c–d

On the other hand, the sameness is qualified, because Socrates feels that some "long and difficult" explanations, mainly concerning radical innovations in philosophical education, have not yet been ventured. Much as he hesitated to talk about women and children when designing the *politeia* earlier, Socrates now contends that some other topics were "not sufficiently clarified" because he was afraid of being rebuked (οὐχ ἱκανῶς, εἶπον, ἐδηλώθη, 497d–e). Socrates' words are striking for the directness with which he names Adeimantus a lawgiver, putting him in the same position as a philosopher-ruler. Nevertheless, whereas he was able to act as the founder of a city-state in conversation, enacting a *politeia* in reality would require "something" else (*ti*) besides Adeimantus. In Adeimantus' view, a plan already exists: he actually did help to design an ideal *politeia*. Socrates, hedging his own view of the existing plan, does not criticize the conversation's achievement (its contents) directly so much as raise meta-conversational reservations about its conduct.

In short, Socrates is saying that more needs to be said. The inadequacy of the conversation's *politeia* lies in the need for more explanation. This is a digressive movement of revision, in which the conversation must turn back and continue to explain itself. Using the optative mood—something "would" be needed in the city—Socrates, as he very often does, limits his opinion to a condition, a possibility, or a potential state of affairs. The uncertain mood is compounded by the indefinite pronoun *ti* 'something', the vagueness of which leaves Adeimantus out of the revised plan. And so the current discussion changes its course, if not quite leaving behind the existing but insufficiently developed plan, then reenvisioning it enough so that it is now once again more potential than real. Socrates reassures Adeimantus that he will again do his best to explain what had been neglected (497e).

A short while later in the conversation, the philosopher-ruler takes his proper place as an ideal legislator, and the speakers try to defend against imagined opponents who would doubt his worthiness. Socrates asks Adeimantus:

ἀλλ' ἐὰν δὴ αἴσθωνται οἱ πολλοὶ ὅτι ἀληθῆ περὶ αὐτοῦ <u>λέγομεν</u>, χαλεπανοῦσι δὴ τοῖς φιλοσόφοις καὶ ἀπιστήσουσιν ἡμῖν <u>λέγουσιν</u> ὡς οὐκ ἄν ποτε ἄλλως εὐδαιμονήσειε πόλις, εἰ μὴ αὐτὴν διαγράψειαν οἱ τῷ θείῳ <u>παραδείγματι</u> χρώμενοι ζωγράφοι;

"Now, if the many perceive that what we say [*legomen*] about this man is true, will they then be harsh with the philosophers and say [*legousi*] they distrust us [when we say] that a city could never be happy unless the painters using the divine model [*paradeigmati*] were to sketch it?"

500d–e

This sentence is difficult to describe because Socrates embeds complex conditional statements inside a conditional question. To put it another way: would not the city's approval depend on its perceiving the truth of what we are saying; namely, that its happiness would depend on philosopher-painters, whose worthiness as legislators would depend on their copying laws from a divine model? The question is rhetorical, but it functions to express likelihood (and not certainty) for the sake of argument, while it also acknowledges how hypothetical the overall proposal is.

Adeimantus asks what "manner" (*tropos*) of sketching Socrates has in mind (501a). In Socrates' response, the conditional question-proposal concerning philosopher-painters becomes the condition or premise for a small hypothetical scenario. Allow me to summarize what Socrates envisages, using the English word *would* to indicate verb forms that are in the optative mood in the Greek. The painters would first make the city into a clean slate; straightaway they would differ from others in starting from scratch (501a). Next they would trace an outline of the regime (501a). Then they would look both toward ideals such as the just, the good, and the moderate, and also toward human beings, and they would put a human image into their plan (501b). And then they would erase one thing and draw another again, until they had made a version of humanity as close to the divine as it could be (501b–c).

Adeimantus then affirms that the resulting drawing "would be ... very good" (καλλίστη γοῦν ἄν, ἔφη, ἡ γραφὴ γένοιτο); and Socrates asks whether the philosopher they had been praising earlier is not this sort of "painter of regimes" (πολιτειῶν ζωγράφος, 501c). Like the Cave scenario we will discuss in the next chapter, the picture Socrates paints here in words is an image about the making of images. The regime painters' portrayal is not a single image, but an evolving sequence of argumentative propositions that relies on imagery. Although the argument comes to seem like a moving picture, it could hardly be called a narrative; instead, it is a type of theoretical discourse, a series of conditional statements, each subordinated to the last, starting from a nonasserted premise (if philosophers drew regimes) and building toward a hypothetical conclusion (they would paint excellent regimes that their citizens might embrace).

Unlike the Cave, however, which is a scenario about what happens in a prison full of false images, the scenario in which the hypothetical philosopher-legislator draws relatively true images is tremendously positive. The resulting drawing of a regime would be a very good drawing indeed, based on "the divine model [*paradeigmati*]" (τῷ θείῳ παραδείγματι χρώμενοι, 500e).

6

Imagining Images in Chains

IN THIS CHAPTER, I approach Plato's scenario of the Cave, starting with some narratological observations and then considering the sequence that moves from the Good through Sun and Divided Line to the Cave. It will take some preparation to reach the Cave itself, but an important part of my argument goes against the typical and long-standing view of the Cave as a sort of fictional narrative. I will suggest that the passage is best considered as a hypothetical scenario, embedded in a sequence of theoretical speculation, and not as an allegory, myth, or literary simile. Insofar as the Cave is a kind of trap for readers, it seduces them into the fixed confines of allegorical interpretation, in which the procedure of making likenesses leaves nowhere else to go.[1]

After situating the Cave scenario in the peculiar narrative discourse of the *Republic*, I make three main points about it. First, I explain the implications of viewing Socrates' description of the Cave as a hypothetical scenario. By *scenario*, I mean a theoretical (and not fictional) sequence of events. While the Cave scenario reflects, and is subordinate to, the passages that precede it—in which Socrates enlists the Sun and the Divided Line to make his notion of the Good more accessible—the scenario itself stands as a chain or stack of hypothetical possibilities and probabilities within the larger sequence, building from one nonasserted premise to the next. It offers a conditional chain of argument that, however outlandish, is rational and literal rather than figurative. My second point is that the Cave is a moment of self-reflection in the *Republic*. The Cave is itself an image, an example of *eikasia*, that tends to hold readers captive. Instead of taking us closer to the idea of the Good, the sun-line-Cave sequence leads several steps away from it. The turning or conversion of prisoners in the Cave, culminating in the murder of the philosopher, is yet another in the series of digressions that structure the entire book so that it avoids reaching a linear endpoint. Hence my third and final point: in its self-referential aspect, the Cave

---

[1] Much of my account of the Cave as a metatextual "trap" and a "mise-en-abîme" is anticipated by Laird 2003, who also notes the "recursiveness" of visual vocabulary in Plato's rhetorical presentation of the scenario.

scenario is essentially a paragon of self-critical reflection, contributing to the undercurrent of caution and equivocation that runs through the entire *Republic*, both as written by the author Plato and as dominated by the character Socrates. The Cave contributes to the methodological thread of thought articulated in language that, in surprising ways, gives preference to ongoing movement as opposed to stopping at an endpoint.

Although the Cave itself is a tomblike torture chamber where prisoners like us would murder their enlightened benefactors, it is nevertheless possible to believe that "the Cave is Plato's most optimistic and beautiful picture of the power of philosophy to free and enlighten."[2] For it is inspiring to imagine ourselves, drawn toward the Good, ascending on "the rough, steep path that leads out of the Cave, up the Line, and into the light of the Sun."[3] But this path reverses and backs out of Socrates' chain of images, in which the Cave is a low point that follows from Socrates' discussion of the Good, which is the highest ideal in Socrates' proposed hierarchy of ideals, paradigms, and Forms. The description of the Cave is a theoretical argument, and its conclusion is a bad one: if these events were to occur, the philosopher would be murdered. And the Cave is explicitly presented as a likeness (*eikōn*) in a context where likenesses and mimesis are subjected to radical criticism.[4]

In explaining these points and anchoring them in the specific language of the text, it is my hope to demonstrate the scenario's extraordinarily self-referential quality. As a powerful example of rhetorical recursion in the book— and a major counterweight to the central image of the sun—the Cave contributes to the pervasive methodological countercurrent that I have been describing, countervailing the idealized version of investigation that also runs through the *Republic* and which is, furthermore, often presumed to be pursued in the service of the Platonic goal of Plato's persuasive efforts. The narrative of the *Republic* has the structure of a journey that begins with a digression and ends with an afterlife. And the conversation throughout the book moves from digression to digression, guided by floating and shifting, buoylike goals rather than by fixed beacons reached as firm conclusions. The Cave counterbalances the sun as a central perspective on human seeking, ultimately raising—but not answering— the question: how could human beings possibly come close to articulating their ideals?

---

[2]   Annas 1981:253.
[3]   Reeves 1988:91.
[4]   See Smith 2007, Laird 2003:16–21; Annas 1981:256–257.

The Cave in Socrates' Fictional Narrative

While the term "narrative" is often used quite loosely, it will be best to reaffirm a definition before turning to the Cave itself. For theorists such as Gérard Genette, a verbal narrative recounts a sequence of events in the voice of a more or less prominent mediator, a narrator who is structurally distinct from the author. Narrative, in this view, exhibits a special temporal structure in which the teller portrays the tale (usually comprising past events) as a connected series of events that have already happened.[5] Less typically, a narrative may report events as currently happening (as when a sports announcer describes a game in progress) or going to happen (as in a prophecy). As concerns fictionality, I follow Dorrit Cohn in maintaining a clear distinction between fictional and historical narrative.[6] Abiding by these categories, I have been calling the whole of Plato's *Republic* a fictional narrative. Nonfictional narratives, such as history books, are recounted by their authors. And however strange the *Republic* may be, it does not raise the kinds of postmodern problems that might in some fundamental way call the adequacy of classical narratology into question.[7] The *Republic* unambiguously presents Socrates telling a story about the previous day, and the fact that Socrates, who historically would have been dead at the time, serves as narrator of Plato's text earmarks the text as fictional.

The length of the *Republic* also makes it unlikely as a verbatim transcript.[8] And the chain of evidence whereby Plato reports what Socrates reported that Socrates and others said on a previous occasion is contrived. Readers are unlikely to construe this narrative as verifiable documentation of the events described. We therefore have good reasons for calling the *Republic* a fictional work of the imagination, featuring the historical Socrates transformed by the author Plato into a fictional character not unlike Virgil in the *Divine Comedy*. Calling the *Republic* a fictional narrative is by no means the same as calling it a novel, but the pretense of fictional narrativity established at the beginning introduces the book as fundamentally mediated and modalized, marked by what narrative theorists call *distance*. I have already linked this distance with the notion of modalization, by which I mean an equivocal mode of discourse that renders thematic statements as possibilities rather than facts, truths, or certainties. Metaphorically expanding grammatical terminology from the level of the sentence to that of discourse, we may describe the global *mood* of the *Republic* as oblique and conditional.

---

[5] Genette 1980:33–34.
[6] Cohn 1999.
[7] "Classical narratology" is a standard designation for the theories of Genette and his peers.
[8] See Ferrari 2010.

At the same time, one of the main things that makes this dialogue (and others) such a *strange* kind of narrative, and quite different from a novel, is that the action is dominated precisely by *dialogue*, the narrative being almost entirely in a mode that Genette identifies as "narrative of words" as opposed to "narrative of events."[9] Instead of mainly recounting various actions performed by characters, Socrates the narrator in the *Republic* primarily reports on what characters said. On the one hand, the utterances presented through reported discourse never quite escape the boundaries of Socrates' narration, retaining their tags of attribution ("he said," "I said") throughout and never quite shifting into unmediated, dramatic speech. One may ignore these nagging reminders of mediation, as C. D. C. Reeve does for reasons of "readability and intelligibility" in his translation of 2004, but this is at the cost of significant texture. As long as our goal is to gather what Plato said in his writings, we must stick to what he actually wrote. Particularly because of the *Republic*'s structure of sequential subordination—whereby Socrates' fictional narrative of events takes us into a fictional narrative of words—I have argued for observing the work as a globally fictional narrative.

On the other hand, the main events in Plato's dialogues are acts of speech and argument; and in the case of the *Republic* such arguably uneventful elements take over after Book 1, with notable exceptions being the embedded narratives concerning Gyges and Er, in which characters *do* lots of things.[10] Keeping in mind the discussion of dominance in my previous chapter, I would also note that almost all fictional narratives contain plenty of nonnarrative, expository elements—static descriptions, comments, claims, arguments, and the like.[11] But the *Republic* seems overwhelmed by expository elements, to the point where its identity as a fictional narrative is threatened. Just as the *Republic* portrays an ideal of ongoing movement (made explicit in Socrates' reluctance to take a stand or position) that struggles to envisage paradigms of discovery, perfection, and knowledge, so too does the book exhibit a struggle in the presentation of ideas in verbal form. These struggles allow us to see standards (conventionalized ideals of perfection) against which to measure both formal features such as digression and thematic concerns such as justice, ideals, and method.

Many readers assume, and some propose—notably Hans Vaihinger—that all imaginary constructs are fictions. But it is useful and commonsensical to observe the difference between theoretical speculation and fictional art, particularly when dealing with literary questions. In Dorrit Cohn's words, summarizing the view of Käte Hamburger, "novels present us with a semblance or

---

9   Genette 1980:169–175, under the heading of "mood" and the subcategory "distance."
10   On eventfulness as a criterion for narrativity, see Schmid 2003.
11   See, e.g., Cohn 1999:14.

illusion (*Schein*) of reality that we don't take in a conditional sense, but that we accept as a reality so long *as* we remain absorbed in it."[12] The Cave scenario, as I will elaborate below, is presented precisely in a conditional sense. Theoretical discourse, which is a brand of expository argumentation, strives for a degree of abstract objectivity that is alien to fictionality and to literature, although it can certainly be found in, and even dominate, works that are otherwise fictional and literary.

Like the *Republic* itself, the Cave is a rather extreme clash between fictional and theoretical discourse. But here my previous concerns are inverted. Whereas an allegory is typically an extended metaphor taking the form of a fictional narrative, the Cave is none of these things.[13] And while the term "allegory" indicates that the text says something other than what it says, allegorical characters and events are understood to translate into transparently stable equivalences, so that an allegorical text has only one correct reading (per allegorical level). Occupying the ultimate position in a sequence of interdependent segments of theoretical speculation, the Cave invites readers to look for this sort of stable meaning, which might stand as a graspable antidote, a cure for our blindness vis-à-vis the Good. In this sense, the Cave holds the temptation of ultimate knowledge by posing as the retrospective key to this puzzle of the Good.[14]

The Greatest Studies

As mentioned in this book's preface, it seems to me that the greatest strangeness of the *Republic* comes mainly from the tension that it builds between posing questions and answering them, by leading readers to seek answers that are not necessarily there. At the same time, the book addresses this tension thematically, as a methodological topic. One of the most striking examples of answers being turned into questions may be seen in the unusual way that the text dwells on the topic of education while continuing to evade—but also to consider and not simply ignore—the human desire for a systematic didactic agenda. That is, even when the thematic focus (the *what*) of the book rests on statements and proposals about education, the methodical treatment (the *how*) of the topic restlessly continues to raise questions about it, and so this raising of questions is highly self-reflective. Socrates' treatment of the Good is the most profound instance of evasion in the *Republic*. He brings up the topic (505a) and

---

[12]   Cohn 1999:6, see 1–17; Hamburger 1993:36–37; and Vaihinger 1924.

[13]   Cf. different views in McCabe 1992; Morgan 2000:202–207; Nightingale 2004:94–98.

[14]   The bibliography listed in Ferarri 2007:501–503 may serve as a starting point for the literature on Sun, Line, and Cave. Cross and Woozley 1964:196–228 provide a helpful overview of key debates. On the Good, see esp. Ferber 1984.

then declines to discuss it directly (506e). As Paul Shorey puts it, "The idea of good is nowhere defined, but its supreme importance and all of its meanings are symbolized in the images of the sun and the cave" (1937:2.xxiii). Shorey's assurance notwithstanding, I would add that the Good is not simply lacking a clear-cut definition in the *Republic*. This supremely important topic is expressly evaded, in a rhetorical move that turns all that follows (by which I mean, in particular, the sequence of Sun, Line, and Cave) into a digression from the Good. In this sense, the Good is an unexpressed, nonasserted premise at the head of a sequence, followed by degraded, metaphorical, subordinate, displaced copies of it. Thus the Good is presented in the text as the ultimate goal and answer—and as a conspicuously unanswered question.[15]

Addressing "The Good As the Supreme Object of Knowledge," R. L. Nettleship sees philosophical education as an important thread of continuity in the *Republic*, linking Books 2–4 with Books 5–7 and also drawing together Books 2–9 (1901:212–213). Nevertheless, "so great an advance" occurs in Books 5–7 "that it looks as if Plato were beginning all over again, and had forgotten or ignored what seemed in the earlier Books to absorb his whole attention" (212). The great digression (which turns away from the absorbing topic of justice at the start of Book 5 and swerves toward the greatest studies) may thus be understood as a corrective revision in the conversation, self-consciously returning to improve on the earlier discussion. But by coming this far and then going back, the conversation only seems to grow longer. As suggested above, this return to the longer way also means revising, again, the benchmarks that were reached when defining justice in the city-state and in the individual. Meanwhile, even more in this revision than before, new priorities seem to lead backward.

Of course, there is nothing unusually recursive about ideas getting revised during a conversation. But Plato's verbal articulation of the conversation's progress forms several interesting perspectives that have little to do with straightforward improvement. For one thing, revising an ideal—an ideal of absolute perfection and completeness—by declaring that it was incomplete after all, leads to the idea of a "better" ideal.[16] Socrates raises this problem explicitly when he reassesses the earlier efforts, in another doubly negative formulation (504c). The problem may be mapped out in the methodological domain of traveling. A foregrounded image of method as a path occurs when Socrates draws closer to the idea of the Good. Reflecting on the method of heuristic conversation pursued thus far, Socrates now wishes to hew strictly to a method that he identifies as a "longer way round [*makrotera ... periodos*]" (μακροτέρα ... περίοδος,

---

[15] Cf. Derrida on "the ellipsis of the sun" (1982:230–244).
[16] Cf. Annas 1981:295 for a comparable observation.

504b). The "longer way round" has been mentioned and avoided before, when the group settled for a merely adequate account of justice in the soul (435d). Socrates now considers their previous findings "lacking in precision" (504b). According to Adeimantus, however, what was said seemed at the time "within measure" and sufficient. Socrates then dismisses this idea of sufficiency and takes a hard line:

ἀτελὲς γὰρ οὐδὲν οὐδενὸς μέτρον. δοκεῖ δ' ἐνίοτέ τισιν ἱκανῶς ἤδη ἔχειν καὶ οὐδὲν δεῖν περαιτέρω ζητεῖν.

"For nothing incomplete [*ateles*] is the measure of anything. But sometimes it seems [*dokei*] to some people to be already sufficient [*hikanōs ekhein*] and to require no further seeking [*zētein*]."

504c

In the context of discussing the earlier discussion, Socrates' swipe at those unspecified people who sometimes compromise too soon leaves room for his fellow investigators to save face by revising their past acceptance, while Adeimantus takes the additional step of deploring a weakness that afflicts some unspecified people.

But the lack of specificity in Socrates' complaint extends beyond the people involved and allows us to glimpse a more general problem. By dwelling on some evocative words here, we may better understand the implications of Socrates' criticism (which is, obliquely, a criticism of the conversation he has been leading). The first of the two sentences just quoted leaves no room for mere sufficiency: according to Socrates, an approach that is *atelēs* 'not (*a-*) complete (*teleios*)' is worthless when it comes to the highest studies. It would leave promising conditions unfulfilled. In this part of the *Republic*, Socrates is turning his attention to the Good as a *telos* ('completion, end, fulfillment', e.g. 504d, cf. 505d–e), and his revised standard of completeness and perfection casts a dubious light not only on earlier findings (such as definitions) but also on earlier standards (such as paradigms) that were beacons guiding the investigation. Some people, ignorant of the incompleteness of their knowledge and complacent in their opinions, see no need for further seeking. The Greek expression translated as "to be already sufficient," combined with an idiom that means something like "it seems" or "they think," conveys two aspects of the problem. As an adverb used with the verb *ekhō* 'to have, hold', *hikanōs* 'sufficiently' describes a state of affairs. Deriving from the verb *hikanō* 'to come to (a place)', *hikanōs* here designates an approach that has reached an endpoint, a static holding pattern of sufficiency. One might also note the connotation of possession introduced by *ekhō* 'to have, hold), which becomes explicit in an upcoming contrast between the everyday possession of goods and the philosophical grasp of the Good (505a–e).

And right before declining to give an account of the Good, Socrates suggests that "men who opine something true without knowledge" are like "blind men traveling [*poreuomenōn*] the right road [*hodon*]" (ἦ δοκοῦσί τί σοι τυφλῶν διαφέρειν ὁδὸν ὀρθῶς πορευομένων οἱ ἄνευ νοῦ ἀληθές τι δοξάζοντες; 506c). Glaucon, understanding that Socrates is on the verge of confessing his own blindness, urges Socrates to "go through" (*dierkhomai*) the Good: "Do not stand away [*aposteis*] when you are, as it were, at the end [*telei*]" (ὥσπερ ἐπὶ τέλει ὢν ἀποστῇς, 506d). The length and circuitousness of the way toward the Good, which is a *periodos* 'round, around (*peri-*) + way (*hodos*)', emphasizes its forbidding distance, which is also reflected in the verb *aphistēmi* (*apo-* 'away, far from' + *histēmi* 'stand').

A Series of Explanatory Comparisons

Unwilling to discuss the Good per se, Socrates instead embarks on a series of comparisons. He starts by likening the Good to the sun (506e–509b), but in making this comparison, which is often called a simile, Socrates embeds two other metaphors within it. "I'm willing to tell what appears [*phainetai*] a child [*ekgonos*] of the Good and most similar [*homoiotatos*] to it" (ὃς δὲ ἔκγονός τε τοῦ ἀγαθοῦ φαίνεται καὶ ὁμοιότατος ἐκείνῳ, λέγειν ἐθέλω, 506e), says Socrates. Only a little later will it dawn on Glaucon that Socrates is talking about the sun (508a). In my opinion, *simile* is a misleadingly literary term for this comparison, given that Socrates is offering a theoretical explanation. Similarly, if a physicist were to tell us that electrons in an atom are like moons orbiting a planet, we would be unlikely to call the comparison a simile.

While delaying the appearance of the sun, however, Socrates teases his listeners with a sort of riddle: the Good is most like something that appears to be a child of the Good. The similarity of Good to sun is thus complicated by a metaphor in which the Good shines like the sun (*phainō* literally = 'comes to light'; "often of the rising of heavenly bodies" [LSJ]) but appears like a child. So the child initially stands in for the sun just as the sun will stand in for the Good. The metaphor also explains the similarity as a kind of dependence: the Good is to the sun as a parent is to a child. Glaucon pushes the metaphor further by calling the narrative of the father a financial debt that will have to be paid later, while Socrates punningly replies that the "interest" (*tokos*, which can also mean 'child, offspring') will have to do for now (507a). The financial metaphor expands on the familial one; and with each turn of metaphor the argument entails a further image (an offspring or copy), a step of subordination, degradation, digression, and debt that takes us a greater *distance* from the original.[17]

For the sake of greater clarity, it is worth reviewing a basic problem of metaphor that figures prominently in Socrates' elaboration of similes about the Good. Our traditional notion of metaphor becomes inadequate when Socrates ascribes literal existence, a higher Reality, to invisible objects, objects that we today call metaphysical, because they are conceived of as existing beyond the physical realm. In order to explain the idea of the Good, Socrates makes a well-known distinction between two fundamental kinds of objects that can be investigated by the soul: real things, which are "seen [*horasthai*] but not intellected [*noeisthai*]," and *ideas* 'Forms', which are intellected but unseen realities (καὶ τὰ μὲν δὴ <u>ὁρασθαί</u> φαμεν, <u>νοεῖσθαι</u> δ' οὔ, τὰς δ' αὖ <u>ἰδέας νοεῖσθαι</u> μέν, <u>ὁρᾶσθαι</u> δ' οὔ, 507b–c). By this point in the *Republic*, the discussion assumes a familiarity with this distinction, and it is implicit in earlier comments made by Socrates as well. Scholars are understandably apt to say that Socrates must resort to metaphorical or mythical language in order to talk about metaphysical Realities such as the Idea of the Good and the Form of Justice. (*Idea* and *eidos* both mean 'form, kind, appearance', although Socrates hints that the Good is in some ways beyond being entirely [509b].)[18] Yet the burden of language in the dilemma of describing metaphysical entities is not to replace them with figurative versions but rather to describe a theoretical Reality. It is for this reason that I would prefer not to call the comparison between the Good and the sun a literary simile. Socrates is saying quite literally that, of all the things in the physical world, the Good is most like the Sun. He could hardly say otherwise, given that the notion of seeing saturates the entire epistemological vocabulary of the Greeks, making the sun a profoundly overdetermined image.

In Socrates' comparison, he stresses that the sun is superior to sight; Glaucon calls the sun the "cause" of sight that is "seen by sight itself" (αἴτιος δ' ὢν αὐτῆς ὁρᾶται ὑπ' αὐτῆς ταύτης, 508b).[19] Thus he starts to describe the proportions of a complex hierarchy—in which effects are subordinated to their causes—that will soon inform the Divided Line. Difficulties of interpretation notwithstanding, we may agree that the visible "region" (*topos* 'place') is subordinate to the intelligible

---

[17] Cf. Derrida 1983:81–83.

[18] So too, the main Greek verb for knowing, *oida* 'to know', is a perfect-tense form of *horaō* 'to see'.

[19] Brann observes: "What is characteristically Socratic about the Sun Image (on which the Divided Line is a gloss) is that it is reflexive, an image of imaging. But more than that, in presenting the sun as an image of the principle of wholeness, Socrates shows not only how imaging itself comes about but also how that particular kind of philosophical imaging which makes the Whole appear as *embedded within itself* is possible—how we can see the Good from within *recursively*, as a likeness of itself. This aspect of the imagery of the *Republic* is reflected also in the central visual image of the closing myth, the Myth of Er" (2004:206, my emphasis).

"region"; and in the Divided Line, likenesses within each of these two realms will be subordinate to originals. Socrates explains the sun as "the offspring of the Good, which the Good begot in a proportion [*analogon*] with itself" (τὸν τοῦ ἀγαθοῦ ἔκγονον, ὃν τἀγαθὸν ἐγέννησεν <u>ἀνάλογον</u> ἑαυτῷ, ὅτιπερ αὐτὸ, 508b). The hierarchy is growing increasingly complicated here, with Socrates using the metaphor of the child (which, to repeat, is already, as a stand-in for the sun, embedded in the comparison of the Good to the sun, in which the sun is a stand-in for the Good) in order to nest analogous categories inside one another: the dependence of the visible on the sun is itself subordinate to the dependence of the Forms on the overarching Idea of the Good.

And in the larger sequence of explanations following in the footsteps of the Good, the Divided Line depends on the proportions used to explain the image of the Sun. Having exclaimed that the Good, in Socrates' account, is a profound "excess," Glaucon must encourage Socrates to continue "going through [*diexiōn*] the comparison [*homoiotēta*] with the Sun" (τὴν περὶ τὸν ἥλιον <u>ὁμοιότητα</u> αὖ <u>διεξιών</u>, 509c). Meanwhile, the theoretical comparison that Socrates is making is coming to be more and more *about* resemblances, and these resemblances are primarily methodological. Each region (*topos* 'place')—the realm of the visible and the realm of the intelligible—is part of a map that describes the world as it can, in practice and in theory, be known. (In fact, the Good and the sun are now both said "to rule as a king" [509b] over their respective regions, a small touch that emphasizes the vastness of this hierarchy, where even philosopher-rulers would themselves submit to ever higher powers and their states would owe allegiance to a yet higher order.)

Using the Divided Line, Socrates explains the relationship between the two regions in terms of likenesses (509d–510b). As indicated in Socrates' earlier remarks about the sun, the visible region is, proportionally, a version of the intelligible region. Each region has two parts. The first part of the visible region contains "images" (*eikōn*) such as shadows and reflections, and each such visible image "is like" (*eoika*) a physical thing in the other part. Socrates introduces a human soul into his description of the intelligible region:

ἧι τὸ μὲν αὐτοῦ τοῖς τότε μιμηθεῖσιν ὡς <u>εἰκόσιν</u> χρωμένη ψυχὴ <u>ζητεῖν</u> ἀναγκάζεται ἐξ ὑποθέσεων, οὐκ ἐπ' <u>ἀρχὴν πορευομένη</u> ἀλλ' ἐπὶ <u>τελευτήν</u>.

"In one part of it, a soul, using as images [*eikosin*] the things that were previously imitated, is compelled to investigate [*zētein*] on the basis of hypotheses, making its way [*poreuomenē*] not to a beginning [*arkhēn*] but to an end [*teleutēn*]...."

510b

For the purposes of my analysis, three things about this difficult passage deserve mention. The first is the recursive interdependence of the two regions. The same things that were physical objects in the visible region are here merely images. Hence in the larger hierarchy the shadowy and reflected images are like the physical objects; the physical objects are like the intelligible objects; and the intelligible objects are like the Forms, which are intelligible by virtue of the Good—all in a theoretical hierarchy of likeness, which is being described by Socrates in a hierarchy of verbal likenesses.

Second, when a human soul enters the picture, we are now talking about methods of investigation as well as the relationships between objects of knowledge. Which brings us to a third point: what ultimately interests Socrates here is the journey of investigation.[20] In the part of the intelligible region just described, the soul must proceed by an inferior route: in the final part of the diagram, the soul is "making [*poioumenē*] its methodical journey [*methodon*]" (τὴν μέθοδον ποιουμένη, 510b) by relying solely on the Forms. Socrates emphasizes that this superior manner of investigation does not reach an end (*teleutē*) but goes "toward an unhypothesized [*anupotheton*] beginning [*arkhēn*]" (ἐπ' ἀρχὴν ἀνυπόθετον, 510b). This paradoxical phrase articulates an endpoint as a starting point, thereby summing up the *Republic*'s paradox of Socratic investigation in a single ideal toward which one travels, from secure suppositions, at the same time that one travels from it toward secure conclusions.

Socrates and then Glaucon also associate superior intellection with a special method of "dialectic" (*dialegomai* 'to converse, discuss'), a procedure whereby "discourse" (*logos*) can understand intelligible objects by moving beyond the hypotheses or assumptions that ground opinion (511b–d). The participants in the current conversation do not seem to view their own dialogue as an example of this special dialectic, but their own investigation of the Good is nonetheless a version—an all-too-human reflection, perhaps—of the greatest studies. By investigating the topic of investigating the Good, the conversation recalled by Socrates in the *Republic* passes its highest point of knowledge just when it approaches a depth of recursion that leads into the Cave. The spatial orientation of Socrates' sequence of images, going from the light of the sun to the darkness of a Cave where the sun will be lost from view, is confirmed in Socrates' overview of the faculties in the soul that correspond to the four types of knowledge portrayed in the Divided Line. Intellection (*noēsis*) is located in the "highest" (*anō*, superlative) quarter of the line; whereas the faculty called *eikasia*, which

---

[20] Cross and Woozley: "We might say that the Line is a map of the country through which the human mind must travel as it progresses from a low degree of intelligence to the highest, while the allegory of the Cave pictures to us the actual journey through the country mapped out in the Line" (1964:208).

comprehends those images most remote from the Good, is at the bottom of the line (511d–e).

Self-Reflection in the Cave

The Cave, in my analysis, is a paragon of self-reflection and rhetorical distancing. Like the makers of political paradigms (472d–e), the prisoners in the Cave are described by Socrates in a sequence of hypothetical statements. The human figures in the sequence (prisoners, puppeteers, visiting philosophers) are said to do things, and the description becomes an extended scenario. As it was with the regime painters, the building of the scenario is punctuated by interruptions from other speakers, frustrating our desire to see the scenario as a smooth and gapless moving picture.

Socrates introduces the initial image of the Cave after summing up the proportions of the divided line.

> μετὰ ταῦτα δή, εἶπον, <u>ἀπείκασον</u> τοιούτῳ πάθει τὴν ἡμετέραν φύσιν παιδείας τε πέρι καὶ ἀπαιδευσίας. <u>ἰδὲ</u> γὰρ ἀνθρώπους οἷον ἐν καταγείῳ οἰκήσει σπηλαιώδει, ἀναπεπταμένην πρὸς τὸ φῶς τὴν <u>εἴσοδον</u> ἐχούσῃ <u>μακρὰν</u> παρὰ πᾶν τὸ σπήλαιον, ἐν ταύτῃ ἐκ παίδων ὄντας ἐν δεσμοῖς καὶ τὰ σκέλη καὶ τοὺς αὐχένας, ὥστε <u>μένειν</u> τε αὐτοὺς εἴς τε τὸ <u>πρόσθεν</u> μόνον <u>ὁρᾶν</u>, κύκλῳ δὲ τὰς κεφαλὰς ὑπὸ τοῦ δεσμοῦ ἀδυνάτους περιάγειν, φῶς δὲ αὐτοῖς πυρὸς <u>ἄνωθεν</u> καὶ <u>πόρρωθεν</u> καόμενον <u>ὄπισθεν</u> αὐτῶν, μεταξὺ δὲ τοῦ πυρὸς καὶ τῶν δεσμωτῶν <u>ἐπάνω ὁδόν</u>, παρ' ἣν <u>ἰδὲ</u> τειχίον παρῳκοδομημένον, ὥσπερ τοῖς θαυματοποιοῖς <u>πρὸ</u> τῶν ἀνθρώπων πρόκειται τὰ παραφράγματα, <u>ὑπὲρ</u> ὧν τὰ θαύματα δεικνύσιν.

"Next then ... make a likeness of [*apeikason*] our nature in its education and want of education, likening it to a condition of the following kind. See [*ide*] human beings as though they were in an underground cavelike dwelling with its entryway [*eisodon*], a long [*makran*] one, open to the light across the whole width of the cave; they are in it from childhood with their legs and necks in bonds so that they are fixed [*menein*], seeing [*horan*] only in front of [*prosthen*] them, unable because of the bond to turn their heads all the way around; their light is from a fire burning above [*anothen*] at a distance [*porrothen*] behind [*opisthen*] them; between the fire and the prisoners there is an upward path [*epano hodos*], along which see [*ide*] a wall, built like the partitions puppet handlers set in front of [*pro*] the human beings and over [*huper*] which they show the puppets."

514a–b

So Socrates' Divided Line leads into an elaborate and extended "image" or "likeness" (*eikōn*, 515a, 517a]). Increasing the rhetorical complexity of image-making here, Socrates uses an imperative, asking his audience to make the likeness, as though each viewer should make a version or copy of the image that Socrates is describing. The Greek verb *apeikazō* 'to form a likeness, copy, compare with' (from the same family as *eikazō* 'to make a likeness' and *eikōn* 'likeness') strongly links the conversational procedure of likening to *eikasia,* the just-mentioned kind of knowledge that occupies the lowest part of the Divided Line.

It is crucial, I believe, that this comparison is to be made between "our" human nature and the condition or experience of the prisoners found in the Cave. Even as we do the likening, we human readers, along with Glaucon and Socrates himself, constitute a term in the comparison. This is stressed when Glaucon says that the image (*eikōn*), and the prisoners, are strange (*atopos* 'not [*a*-] a place [*topos*]'), and Socrates replies that the prisoners are like (*homoios*) us (515a). We are therefore implicated, involved, and reflected in the unfolding events that ensue from the initial image.

Many of the details described in the image evoke concerns that have been developed over the course of the dialogue, and the elaborate orientation of elements in the Cave echoes the disorientation observed in the *Republic*'s opening scene. Relevant themes implicated in methodological questions include the use of images as likenesses, images as shadows and reflections, the length of the path and the distance from the light, the theme of sight, and the struggle between moving and remaining in place. Examples of recursion are rife: use an image to liken us to prisoners who are captivated by images; see prisoners seeing; investigate the path of investigation.

A single sentence, complex and meandering, sets the scene. The aorist imperative "see" (*ide*, 514a) is followed by a string of seemingly subordinate participles that at times characterize the inhabitants and at other times the Cave. The description floats in a kind of timeless present, without finite verbs or distinct tense markers. Although translators are inevitably compelled to use numerous finite verb forms in English, in Greek the elements of the image are simply *there*. How these sights depend upon our seeing is emphasized by the repetition later in the sentence of the aorist imperative (*ide*, 514b); the result is a strange concurrence of linguistic indirection and imaginary, timeless presence before our eyes. When Socrates pauses, Glaucon replies in the present indicative, "I see" (*horō*). While the tenses and moods are perfectly fitting, we should note that the image is not (yet) conditional, unreal, or even nonreal; Glaucon is, in theory, seeing the picture constructed by Socrates. That is, although he exists here in a realm of historical fiction, Glaucon is responding as a listener-reader to the nonfictional, ahistorical image. Accordingly, there is no grammatical indication of unreality. Instead, the grammatical form is *indirect* in both syntax and mood.

The successive segments of the sentence weave back and forth between the people in the Cave and the Cave itself. And the sense of an unstable focus pervades the whole sentence. In the middle of the sentence, we find an explanatory result clause containing two infinitives, "remain" and "see." More participles follow until the end of the sentence, where a simile between the little wall in the Cave and partitions used by puppeteers contains two finite verbs. Though the cave image is itself introduced as the simile's qualified metaphorical vehicle, a vague and qualified condition; the puppeteers' partition is a metaphorical vehicle used to describe the Cave. As such, the puppeteering wall, presumably a reality familiar to the Greeks and therefore described with the gnomic present tense, becomes a secondary or subsimile; an internal wall, fittingly wedged into a convoluted syntactical construct.

Socrates is presumably using similes because a familiar image can help us to grasp an abstraction. And this *eikōn* 'likeness' of the Cave is inviting us to practice *eikasia*, even though Socrates has recently denigrated the use of images. Thus the methodological rhetoric (and vocabulary) of the Line is embedded in the Cave. But if the puppet partition helps to explain the peculiar cave wall, it puts *us* at a double remove from the aspects of human nature that this whole complex of imagery is supposed to illuminate. The sentence begins with the narrator's telling us what was said in the past, and ends with a comparison in the gnomic tense of timeless theoretical truth. This progression hardly provides a definitive model for what Plato is doing in the passage as a whole, but it does exhibit a peculiar imbalance between what is fiction posing as fact (as in "I said this yesterday") and what is fact presented in a figurative amplification (like puppeteers' partitions).

Conditions in the Cave

After Socrates has asked his listeners to make a likeness of (*apeikazō*) the image or likeness (*eikōn*) of prisoners in a Cave, he explains why he thinks the prisoners are like (*homoios*) us: "For in the first place, do you suppose [*oiei*] such men would have seen [*heōrakenai*] anything of themselves and one another other than the shadows ... ?" (τοὺς γὰρ τοιούτους πρῶτον μὲν ἑαυτῶν τε καὶ ἀλλήλων <u>οἴει</u> ἄν τι <u>ἑωρακέναι</u> ἄλλο πλὴν τὰς σκιὰς, 515a). Socrates' image of prisoners in a cave works something like a mirror insofar as it gives its viewers an opportunity to see an image of themselves; the prisoners in the image are like its viewers (us). Yet what makes the people in the image like us is, strangely enough, their inability to see themselves, which suggests that we are going to have trouble seeing the image as it is. It is shadowy, ominous, and chthonic. Socrates explains his comparison between prisoner-viewers and us-viewers by asking Glaucon to treat the initial image of the Cave as a hypothetical assumption—based on the situation described, further conclusions can be drawn. The image thus acts as an understood conditional clause (which is in fact supplied in Glaucon's response: "If they should have been compelled [optative mood] to keep their heads motionless," εἰ ἀκινήτους γε τὰς κεφαλὰς ἔχειν ἠναγκασμένοι, 515a), while the verb *oiomai* 'to suppose' introduces a conclusion.[21] And with this conditional question, Socrates establishes the underlying grammatical and rhetorical structure of the Cave scenario, which may be viewed as a long chain of future-less-vivid ("should–would") conditions, moving from one supposition to the next. The entire chain of reasoning constitutes a thought experiment.[22] Through conversation, the speakers develop a speculative account of what would happen, in theory, if the imagined state of affairs were to exist. (And strangeness notwithstanding, Glaucon fully entertains the possibility that such a cave full of prisoners could, in theory, exist; if only for the sake of conversation.)

Socrates continues to ask questions and draw conclusions, and in each instance he seeks Glaucon's confirmation: *If* the prisoners *should* be able to converse (*dialegomai*, 515b), do you not believe they *would* hold such and such? *If* the prison *should* have an echo, do you suppose the prisoners *would* believe such and such? Then surely they *would* hold such and such … (515c). This is how Socrates articulates the entire scenario (514a–517a); a fuller summary would be tedious. The prisoners do things and have various things done to them, and they even converse while deep in their Cave, which is embedded deep in the conversation recounted by Socrates in the Platonic dialogue. But unlike the tale of Er, in which voices proliferate and echo forth as reports from beyond the grave, the long scenario is not a recounting of anything. It is an account propelled by calculative thinking. Neither Socrates' companions nor we readers are invited to believe that these events have happened, are happening, or will happen; instead, the scenario has us imagine and consider what would happen under

---

[21] The verb form translated "would have seen" is an infinitive (*heōrakenai*) accompanied by the modal particle *an*, which indicates the optatival sense of the infinitive.

[22] "A 'thought experiment' is an attempt to draw instruction from a process of hypothetical reasoning that proceeds by eliciting the consequences of an hypothesis which, for aught that one actually knows to the contrary, may well be false. It consists in reasoning from a supposition that is not accepted as true—perhaps is even known to be false—but is assumed provisionally in the interests of making a point or resolving a conclusion" (Rescher 1991:31).

certain specified conditions. The events described are striking and memorable, but the cognitive process holding them together is one of rational acceptance, subsequent events in the scenario being entirely dependent on conditions that were accepted previously.

All of these suppositions, each one subordinated under the last, recede toward a devastatingly profound conclusion: "And if they [the Cave dwellers] should be somehow able to get their hands on and kill the man who attempts to release and lead upward [*anagein*], wouldn't they kill him?" (καὶ τὸν ἐπιχειροῦντα λύειν τε καὶ <u>ἀνάγειν</u>, εἴ πως ἐν ταῖς χερσὶ δύναιντο λαβεῖν καὶ ἀποκτείνειν, ἀποκτεινύναι ἄν; 517a). This question is nothing like the conclusion of a fictional narrative, and this central conclusion's theoretical power—the likelihood that something so shocking could possibly happen in practice—is anachronistically confirmed by allusion to the historical execution of Socrates. With such an extraliterary allusion, this hypothetical scenario in a theoretical sequence in a fictional text draws attention to itself as authored by Plato, and Plato's fictional character Socrates draws attention to himself as a version of a historical figure who is here theorizing by means of comparisons. The self-awareness of the Cave scenario closes in on itself, emphasizing that Socrates, unable to reach the Good in conversation, has instead led us to a potentially fatal depth of theoretical likenesses. Having predicted his own murder as a theoretical likelihood, Socrates tells Glaucon to connect "this image [*eikona*] as a whole with what was said before" (ταύτην τοίνυν, ἦν δ᾽ ἐγώ, τὴν <u>εἰκόνα</u>, ὦ φίλε Γλαύκων, προσαπτέον ἅπασαν τοῖς ἔμπροσθεν λεγομένοις, 517a–b). In order to move forward, Socrates looks backward.

The Cave scenario radically tests the conceptual boundaries of discourse and conversational practice. Socrates introduced the Sun as a way to get around and past the ineffable and elusive Idea of the Good, but this detour has led downward, away from the Sun and under the ground. Located in a theoretical sequence in a fictional depiction of a heuristic conversation, and itself a conversational detour embedded in the larger, ongoing conversation, the scenario is a sublime *mise-en-abîme*, where methodical discourse questions itself.[23] The scenario may well serve the ends of the conversation, helping us to imagine a path out of our world of shadows. But it is hardly a pretty picture and it is far from the end of the book.

---

[23] On the Cave as mise-en-abîme, cf. Laird 2003, esp. 27.

Afterword

IT IS GENERALLY ASSUMED that Plato, while cultivating and perpetuating Socrates' legacy of ostensible ignorance in the most important matters, writes as a knower with a persuasive, didactic agenda. Some see Plato promoting specific theoretical doctrines; others figure that Plato is guiding us to adopt practices that will in turn lead us to find truths he has already found. Especially insofar as the dialogues portray goal-oriented investigations, Plato is viewed as an author who guides us to receive and possess—to get—a message he already has fixed in mind. At the same time, Plato's literary art has been celebrated throughout the history of Platonism for its inspiring beauty. Because expressions of appreciation for that beauty can in fact be impressionistic, dismissive, or condescending, it has proved difficult for today's scholars to maintain a balance between acknowledging Plato's artistry and assessing the rigor of his thought—especially since most readers of Plato are looking for content in the form of authorial assertions. Art as such, by the definition that emerges from these readers' interpretive conceptions of content, does not provide the sort of straightforward answers that they desire and demand. Hence the recent drive to explain Plato's art as a technical art of rhetoric, one that extrudes content *through* form.

I have argued that readers regularly, if haphazardly, make a commonsensical choice between expository and literary modes of reading. These modes correspond to different desires and purposes, and in their modern incarnations also distinguish philosophy from literature. If there is a false dichotomy here, it is the separation of aesthetic pleasure from intellectual edification, as though ideas had to be separated out from language and pinned down in a systematic catalog before they might be of interest and value. Such a dichotomy risks losing the wonder observed by Aristotle in the human desire, exhibited in the drive of physical sensation [*aisthēsis*], to know about the highest things.[1] Plato's

---

[1] *Metaphysics* 982a–b, where Aristotle also touches on the idea of the supreme good as a telos in and of itself. Cf. *De Anima* 402a on the beauty and value of knowledge of the greatest and most wondrous things, and *Nicomachean Ethics* 1094a on the good as a telos sought for its own sake, regardless of idle talk about the regression of goals underlying goals ad infinitum.

language is essentially provisional, the promise of the dialogues being sustained by a relentless, visionary sense of wonder. Be that as it may, to appreciate how thought and language emerge together in the reading of a text does not require that we simply abandon ourselves to fuzzy emotional impressions.[2] Plato's dialogues are permeated by complex and questioning thought and language, where questions have no less beauty—and no less value—than do the answers proposed by his speaking characters. Is there any doubt that Plato's aesthetic is the height of intellectualism?

Many of the major problems posed by the *Republic* can be understood as impasses, navigated by means of rhetorical tropes that allow the book to keep going. The journey to reach ideals is thus one of asymptotic approximation; a journey of perpetual approach. In a conversation that sets out with the end goal of perfection in mind, endings devolve into beginnings, while verbal displacements proliferate whereby the ideal world becomes the reality, theory becomes practice, method (path) becomes topic (place), and conversation becomes philosophy. One significant way that Plato idealizes conversation is through tropes of recursion that describe an endless journey. Endlessness here need not be infinite regression in a strictly logical sense. Instead, chains of digression, hearsay, and conditional speculation evoke the sublime. As well as being the highest object of knowledge, the Good is the acme of this sublime—incalculable, ineffable, and blinding—so that we must turn away from it in order to see it better.

---

[2] See Klein's excoriation of modern aesthetic approaches to Plato that lose sight of the text's pedagogical task (1965:20).

Glossary of Key Greek Words

G REEK WORDS are transliterated and given in the forms they have as head-words in LSJ (e.g. *heuriskō* 'to find', literally 'I find'). Other forms of the same word found in the text are noted under the headword unless they differ significantly. These words are meant as signposts for those who do not read Greek, and the definitions simply identify some relevant semantic ranges.

adikia 'injustice'

agapaō 'to be pleased, content' (*agapēseis* 'you will be content', *agapēsomen* 'we shall be content')

agō 'to lead, conduct' (*agousa*, pl. *agontes* 'leading, conducting')

aisthēsis 'sensation'

akouō 'to hear' (*akousai* [inf.] 'to hear')

alēthē, alēthēs 'true'

an (functions as a modal, conditional particle)

anabainō 'to ascend'; *anabasis, -in* 'ascent'

anaballō 'to postpone' (*anabalesthai* [inf.] 'to postpone')

anagō 'to lead upward' (*anagein* [inf.] 'to lead upward')

analogos, -on 'proportionate; in proportion'

anankē 'necessarily'

angelos, -on 'messenger'

anō 'up, upward'; *anōthen* 'above'

anodos, -on 'upward path' (= *anō* + *hodos*)

anupothetos, -on 'unhypothesized'

apeikazō 'to make a likeness of, compare' (*apeikason* 'form!')

apeimi 'to go away' (*apēimen* 'we were going away', *apiontes* 'going away') *aphistēmi* 'to stand away from' (*apostēis* 'stand away!') (= *apo-* + *histēmi* 'stand')

apisteō 'to disbelieve, distrust, doubt' (*apistounta* 'doubting', *apistēsetai* 'he will doubt') (= *a-* 'not' + *pisteuō*)

apo- 'away from, back again'

apodidraskō 'to run away' (*apodidraskōn* 'running away')

arkhē, -n 'beginning'

atelēs, -es 'not complete' (= *a-* + *teleios*)

atopos 'strange, out of place'

brakhus 'short'

dei 'it is necessary'

deuro 'here'

dialegomai 'to converse' (*dialexometha* 'we will converse'); *dialogos, -ou* 'conversation'

diapheugō 'to flee through' (= *dia-* 'through' + *pheugō* 'to flee')

dierkhomai 'to go through' (*dielthein* [aor. inf.] 'to go through', *diēlthomen* 'we went through', *dielēluthamen* 'we have gone through', *dielēluthōs*, *diexelthontes* 'having gone through', *diexiōn* 'going through')

dikaiosunē 'justice'

dokeō 'to think, seem' (*dokei, dokō* 'it seems', *dokēi* 'it might seem', *doxaimen* 'we would appear')

*eidō (see *horaō*)

eidos 'form, category'

eikasia 'image, likeness; comparison'

eikōn, -ona 'image, likeness'; *eikazō* 'to make a likeness; compare'

eikos 'likely, probable'

eisodon 'entryway' (= *eis-* 'into' + *hodos*)

ekgonos 'child'

ekhō 'to have, hold' (*ekhein* [inf.] 'to hold', *hexometha* 'we shall hold')

elpis 'hope'

elthein (see *erkhomai*)

engus 'near', *engutata* 'nearest'

epanō 'above'

episkopeō 'to examine' (*episkepsōmetha* 'let us examine')

erkhomai 'to go' (*elthein* [aor. 2 inf.] 'to go', *dielēluthōs* 'having gone through')

exeuriskō 'to find out, discover' (*exēurēkenai* [perf. inf.] 'to have found out') (= *ex-* 'out' + *heuriskō*)

heortazō 'to keep festival or holiday' (*heortasai* [inf.] 'to take a holiday')

heuriskō 'to find' (*heurōmen* 'we shall find', *heurein* [inf.] 'to find', *hēurēkenai* [perf. inf.] 'to have found')

hexō (future of *ekhō*)

hikanō 'to come to (a place)'; *hikanōs* 'sufficiently'

hodos, *-on*, *-ou*; pl. *hodoi* 'path, road, way; journey'

homoiotēs, *-ta* 'resemblance, similarity'; *homoiotatos* 'most similar'

horaō 'to see' (*horō* 'I see', *horasthai* 'to be seen', *horan* 'to see', *heōrakenai* 'to have seen'; *idein* 'to see', *idoimen* 'we would see', *ide* 'see!, imagine!' [from aor. 2. **eidō*])

horos 'definition; boundary, limit; rule, standard, measure; end, aim'

huper 'over'

idea 'form, kind, sort'

isōs 'perhaps'

kados 'jar, urn, box'

katabainō 'to descend' (*katebēn* 'I went down')

katadromē, *-n* 'raid, incursion' (= *kata-* 'down' + *dromos* 'run')

keleuō 'to command'

khalepos (pl. *-a*) 'difficult'

khrē 'it must, one must' (*khrēnai* [inf.] 'it is necessary')

kineō 'to set in motion' (*kineite* 'you set in motion')

legō 'to speak, say' (*legomen* 'we say', *legousi* 'they say')

logos, *-ōi*; pl. *-oi*, *-ous* 'word, discourse, thought'

makros, *-a* 'long', *makrotera* 'longer'

menō 'to remain' (*menein* [inf.] 'to remain')

metastrephō 'to turn round' (*metestraphēn* 'turned round')

methodos, -on 'path of pursuit' (pl. *methodoi, -ōn*) (= *meta-* 'beside, along' + *hodos*)

noeō 'to think, conceive' (*noeisthai* [inf.] 'to think, conceive')

oikade 'homeward'

oiomai, oimai 'to suppose' (*oiei* 'you suppose')

opisthen 'behind, from behind'

paradeigma, -tos, -ti 'model, pattern'

pempō 'to send, conduct, escort' (*epempon* 'they marched')

periodos 'way round, around' (= *peri-* 'around' + *hodos*)

pisteuō 'to believe' (*pisteuontos* 'believing')

phainō 'to make appear; be seen to appear' (*phainetai* 'it appears')

phēmi 'to speak' (*phaimen* (opt.) 'we should say', *phōmen* (subj.) 'let us say')

poieō 'to make, create' (*poieisthai* [inf.] 'to make', *poiēsetai* 'he will make', *poiōmen* 'let us make', *poioumenē* 'making', *epoioumen* 'we were making')

politeia 'political organization'

pompē 'march, procession'

poreia, -ai 'journey'; *poreuō* 'to walk, travel' (*poreuōntai* 'they travel', *poreuomenōn, -ē* 'traveling')

porrōthen 'from a distance'

prattō 'to do, fare' (*prattōmen* 'we will fare')

pro 'in front'

prophētēs 'spokesman'

pros 'toward'

proserkhomai 'to go toward' (*proserkhetai* 'he goes toward')

telos, -ei; *teleutē, -n* 'end, completion, fulfillment'; *teleiōs* 'completely'; *teleutaō* 'to come to an end' (*teleutēsanta* 'coming to an end')

theaomai 'to look at' (*theasasthai* [inf.] 'to watch', *theasaimetha* [opt.] 'we should watch'); *theōria* 'a looking at; sight-seeing trip' *thnēskō* 'to die'

ti 'something'

tokos 'offspring; interest'

tropos, -on, -ōi 'turn; manner'

zēteō 'to seek' (*zētein* [inf.] 'to seek', *zētoumen* 'we seek', *zētēsōmen* 'let us seek', *zētounta*, pl. *tes* 'seeking'); *zētēsis* 'a seeking, investigation', *zētēma* 'something sought'

.

Bibliography

Adam, J. 1902. *The* Republic *of Plato*. 2 vols. London.

Adams, H., ed. 1992. *Critical Theory Since Plato*. Rev. ed. Fort Worth.

Annas, J. 1981. *An Introduction to Plato's* Republic. Oxford.

———. 1996. "Plato." *Oxford Classical Dictionary*, 3rd ed.

———. 1999. *Platonic Ethics, Old and New*. Ithaca.

———. 2000. *Ancient Philosophy: A Very Short Introduction*. Oxford.

Annas, J., and C. Rowe, eds. 2002. *New Perspectives on Plato: Modern and Ancient*. Washington, DC.

Arieti, J. A. 1998. "How to Read a Platonic Dialogue." In *Plato: Critical Assessments*, ed. N. D. Smith, 1:273–286. London.

Aviram, A. F. 2001. "Literariness, Markedness, and Surprise in Poetry." http://www.amitai.com/prose/marked.php.

Bal, M. 2009. *Narratology: Introduction to the Theory of Narrative*. 3rd. ed. Toronto.

Barney, R. 2010. "Platonic Ring-Composition and *Republic* 10." In McPherran 2010:32–49.

Barthes, R. 1986. *The Rustle of Language*. Trans. R. Howard. Oxford.

Beardsley, M. C. 1981. *Aesthetics: Problems in the Philosophy of Criticism*. Indianapolis.

Becker, O. 1937. *Das Bild des Weges und verwandte Vorstellungen im frühgriechischen Denken*. Berlin.

Benardete, S. 1992. *Socrates' Second Sailing: On Plato's* Republic. Chicago.

Blondell, R. 2002. *The Play of Character in Plato's Dialogues*. Cambridge.

Bloom, A. 1968. *The* Republic *of Plato*. New York.

Borges, J. L. 1964. *Labyrinths: Selected Stories and Other Writings*. New York.

Bradford, R. 1997. *Stylistics*. London.

Brann, E. 2004. *The Music of the* Republic: *Essays on Socrates' Conversations and Plato's Writings*. With P. Kalkavage and E. Salem. Philadelphia.

Brooks, C. 1947. *The Well Wrought Urn: Studies in the Structure of Poetry*. San Diego.

Brooks, P. 1984. *Reading for the Plot: Design and Intention in Narrative*. Cambridge, MA.

Burke, K. 1967. "Rhetoric—Old and New." In *New Rhetorics*, ed. M. Steinmann, Jr., 59–76. New York.

———. 1969. *A Grammar of Motives*. Berkeley.

Burnet, J. 1903. *Plato's* Republic. Oxford.

Burnyeat, M. F. 1999. "Utopia and Fantasy: The Practicability of Plato's Ideally Just City." In *Plato 2: Ethics, Politics, Religion, and the Soul*, ed. G. Fine, 297–308. Oxford.

CGEL = Huddleston, R., and G. K. Pullum. 2002. *The Cambridge Grammar of the English Language*. Cambridge.

Chantraine, P. 2009. *Dictionnaire étymologique de la langue grecque: Histoire des mots.* Rev. ed. Paris.

Chatman, S. 1978. *Story and Discourse: Narrative Structure in Fiction and Film*. Ithaca.

———. 1990. *Coming to Terms: The Rhetoric of Narrative and Film*. Ithaca.

Clay, D. 1992. "Plato's First Words." In *Beginnings in Classical Literature*, ed. F. M. Dunn and T. Cole, 113–129. Yale Classical Studies 29. Cambridge.

———. 2000. *Platonic Questions: Dialogues with the Silent Philosopher*. University Park.

Cohn, D. 1999. *The Distinction of Fiction*. Baltimore.

———. 2000. "The Poetics of Plato's *Republic*: A Modern Perspective." *Philosophy and Literature* 24:34–48.

———. 2001. "Does Socrates Speak for Plato? Reflections on an Open Question." *New Literary History* 32:485–500.

Cole, T. 1991. *The Origins of Rhetoric in Ancient Greece*. Baltimore.

Comrie, B. 1985. *Tense*. Cambridge.

Cooper, J. M. 1997. "Introduction." *Plato: Complete Works*. Indianapolis.

Corlett, J. A. 2005. *Interpreting Plato's Dialogues*. Las Vegas.

Crombie, I. M. 1962. *An Examination of Plato's Doctrines*. Vol. 1. London.

Cross, R. C., and A. D. Woozley. 1964. *Plato's* Republic: *A Philosophical Commentary*. London.

Culler, J. 1975. "Linguistic Metaphors in Criticism." In *Structuralist Poetics*, 96–109. Ithaca.

———. 1988. "Interpretations: Data or Goals?" *Poetics Today* 9:275–290.

———. 2002. "The Turns of Metaphor." In *The Pursuit of Signs*, 188–209. Ithaca.

———. 2007. "Commentary: What Is Literature Now?" *New Literary History* 38:229–237.

Dällenbach, L. 1989. *The Mirror in the Text*. Trans. J. Whiteley and E. Hughes. Chicago.

de Man, P. 1973. "Semiology and Rhetoric." *Diacritics* 3:27–33.

Derrida, J. 1983. "Plato's Pharmacy." In *Dissemination*, trans. B. Johnson, 63–171. Chicago.

———. 1984. "White Mythology: Metaphor in the Text of Philosophy." In *Margins: Of Philosophy*, trans. A. Bass, 207–271. Chicago.

Duhoux, Y. 2000. *Le verbe grec ancien: Éléments de morphologie et de syntaxe historiques.* 2nd ed. Louvain-la-Neuve.

Edelstein, L. 1998. "Platonic Anonymity." In Smith 1998, 1:183–200.

Edgington, D. 2008. "Conditionals." *The Stanford Encyclopedia of Philosophy.* Ed. E. N. Zalta. http://plato.stanford.edu/archives/win2008/entries/conditionals/.

Edmunds, L. 2005. "Critical Divergences: New Directions in the Study and Teaching of Roman Literature." *Transactions of the American Philological Association* 135:1–13.

Emlyn-Jones, C., and W. Preddy, eds. 2013. *Plato: Republic.* 2 vols. Cambridge, MA.

Enkvist, N. E. 1985. "Text and Discourse Linguistics, Rhetoric, and Stylistics." In *Discourse and Literature*, ed. T. A. van Dijk, 11–38. Amsterdam.

Ferber, R. 1984. *Platos Idee des Guten.* Sankt Augustin.

Ferrari, G. R. F. 1987. *Listening to the Cicadas: A Study of Plato's* Phaedrus. Cambridge.

———, ed. 2007. *Cambridge Companion to Plato's* Republic. Cambridge.

———. 2010. "Socrates in the *Republic.*" In McPherran 2010:11–31.

Fleischman, S. 1989. "Temporal Distance: A Basic Linguistic Metaphor." *Studies in Language* 13:1–50.

Ford, A. 1992. *Homer: The Poetry of the Past.* Ithaca.

———. 2010. "Sōkratikoi Logoi in Aristotle and Fourth-Century Theories of Genre." *Classical Philology* 105.3:221–235.

Fowler, R. 1996. *Linguistic Criticism.* 2nd ed. Oxford.

Frede, M. 1992. "Plato's Arguments and the Dialogue Form." In Klagge and Smith 1992:201–219.

Freud, S. 1953. *The Standard Edition of the Complete Psychological Works of Sigmund Freud.* Ed. and trans. J. Strachey. Vol. 4 (*The Interpretation of Dreams*, pt. 1). London. Orig. pub. 1900.

Frye, N. 1957. *Anatomy of Criticism: Four Essays.* Princeton.

Fujisawa, N. 1974. "Echein, Metechein, and Idioms of 'Paradeigmatism' in Plato's Theory of Forms." *Phronesis* 19:30–58.

Gallop, D. 2003. "The Rhetoric of Philosophy: Socrates' Swan-Song." In *Plato As Author: The Rhetoric of Philosophy*, ed. A. N. Michelini, 313–332. Leiden.

Genette, G. 1980. *Narrative Discourse: An Essay in Method.* Trans. J. E. Lewin. Ithaca.

———. 1993. *Fiction and Diction.* Trans. C. Porter. Ithaca.

Gill, C. 1979. "Plato's Atlantis Story and the Birth of Fiction." *Philosophy and Literature* 3.1:64–78.

———. 1993. "Plato on Falsehood—not Fiction." In Gill and Wiseman 1993:38–87.

Gill, C., and M. M. McCabe, eds. 1996. *Form and Argument in Late Plato.* Oxford.

Gill, C., and T. P. Wiseman, eds. 1993. *Lies and Fiction in the Ancient World.* Austin.

Goldschmidt, V. 1963. *Les dialogues de Platon.* 2nd ed. Paris.

Gonzalez, F. J., ed. 1995. *The Third Way: New Directions in Platonic Studies.* Lanham.

Goodwin, W. W. 1890. *Syntax of the Moods and Tenses of the Greek Verb.* Philadelphia. Reprint ed. 1992.

Gordon, J. 1999. *Turning Toward Philosophy: Literary Device and Dramatic Structure in Plato's Dialogues.* University Park, PA.

Greetham, D. C. 1994. *Textual Scholarship: An Introduction.* New York.

———. 1999. *Theories of the Text.* Oxford.

Griswold, C. L. 1999. "E Pluribus Unum? On the Platonic 'Corpus.'" *Ancient Philosophy* 19:361–397.

———, ed. 2002. *Platonic Writings/Platonic Readings.* Updated ed. University Park, PA.

Grube, G. M. A., and C. D. C. Reeve. 1992. *Plato:* Republic. Trans. G. M. A. Grube, rev. C. D. C. Reeve. Indianapolis.

Halliwell, S. 1988. *Plato:* Republic 10. Warminster.

———. 2007. "The Life-and-Death Journey of the Soul: Interpreting the Myth of Er." In Ferrari 2007:445-473.

———. 2009. "The Theory and Practice of Narrative in Plato." In *The Content of Narrative Form in Ancient Literature*, ed. J. Grethlein and A. Rengakos, 15–41. Berlin.

———. 2011a. "Antidotes and Incantations: Is There a Cure for Poetry in Plato's *Republic*?" In *Plato and the Poets*, ed. P. Destrée and F.-G. Herrmann, 241–266. Leiden.

———. 2011b. *Between Ecstasy and Truth: Interpretations of Greek Poetics from Homer to Longinus.* Oxford.

Hamburger, K. 1993. *The Logic of Literature.* Trans. M. J. Rose. 2nd, rev. ed. Bloomington.

Hart, R., and V. Tejera, eds. 1997. *Plato's Dialogues: The Dialogical Approach.* Lewiston.

Hawkes, T. 2003. *Structuralism and Semiotics.* 2nd ed. New York.

Heath, M. 2002. *Interpreting Classical Texts.* London.

Hirsch, E. D. 1976. "Objective Interpretation." In *On Literary Intention*, ed. D. Newton-De Molina, 26–54. Edinburgh.

Hollander, J. 2001. *Rhyme's Reason.* New Haven.

Howland, J. 2004. *The* Republic: The Odyssey of Philosophy. Philadelphia.

Irwin, T. 2002. "Reply to David L. Roochnik." In Griswold 2002:194–199.

Jacobs, C. 2008. "Subversions of the Political: Plato's *Republic*." In *Skirting the Ethical*, 45–110. Stanford.

Jakobson, R. 1987. *Language in Literature.* Ed. K. Pomorska and S. Rudy. Cambridge, MA.

Jeffries, L., and D. McIntyre. 2010. *Stylistics.* Cambridge.

Johnson, W. A. 1998. "Dramatic Frame and Philosophic Idea in Plato." *American Journal of Philology* 119:577–598.

Jowett, B., and L. Campbell, eds. 1894. *Plato's* Republic. 3 vols. Oxford.

Kahn, C. H. 1996. *Plato and the Socratic Dialogue: The Philosophical Use of a Literary Form.* Cambridge.

———. 2000. "Response to Griswold." *Ancient Philosophy* 20:189–193.

Kermode, F. 1967. *The Sense of an Ending: Studies in the Theory of Fiction.* New York.

Kindt, T., and H.-H. Müller, eds. 2003. *What is Narratology? Questions and Answers Regarding the Status of a Theory.* Berlin.

Klagge, J. C., and N. D. Smith, eds. 1992. *Methods of Interpreting Plato and His Dialogues. Oxford Studies in Ancient Philosophy.* Oxford.

Klein, J. 1965. *A Commentary on Plato's* Meno. Chicago.

Krämer, H. J. 1990. *Plato and the Foundations of Metaphysics: A Work on the Theory of the Principles and Unwritten Doctrines of Plato with a Collection of the Fundamental Documents.* Ed. and trans. J. R. Catan. Albany.

Kraut, R. 1992. "Introduction to the Study of Plato." In *The Cambridge Companion to Plato*, 1–50. Cambridge.

———. 2009. "Plato." *The Stanford Encyclopedia of Philosophy.* Ed. E. N. Zalta. http://plato.stanford.edu/archives/fall2009/entries/plato/.

Laird, A. 2003. "Death, Politics, Vision, and Fiction in Plato's Cave (After Saramago)." *Arion*, 3rd ser., 10.3:1–30.

Lakoff, G., and M. Johnson. 2003. *Metaphors We Live By.* Chicago.

Lamarque, P., and S. H. Olsen. 1994. *Truth, Fiction and Literature: A Philosophical Perspective.* Oxford.

Lamm, J. A. 2000. "Schleiermacher as Plato Scholar." *Journal of Religion* 80:206–239.

Lejeune, P. 1989. *On Autobiography.* Ed. P. J. Eakin. Trans. K. Leary. Minneapolis.

LSJ = Liddell, H. G., R. Scott, and H. Stuart Jones, eds. *Greek-English Lexicon.* 9th ed. Oxford.

Lyons, J. 1968. *Introduction to Theoretical Linguistics.* Cambridge.

———. 1977. *Semantics.* Vol. 2. Cambridge.

Marshall, D. G. 1992. "Literary Interpretation." In *Introduction to Scholarship in Modern Languages and Literatures*, ed. J. Gibaldi, 159–182. 2nd ed. New York.

Matthews, P. H. 1997. *Concise Oxford Dictionary of Linguistics.* Oxford.

Maynard, J. 2009. *Literary Intention, Literary Interpretation, and Readers.* Toronto.

McCabe, M. M. 1992. "Myth, Allegory and Argument in Plato." In *The Language of the Cave*, ed. A. Barker and M. Warner, 47–67. Edmonton.

———. 2008. "Plato's Ways of Writing." In *The Oxford Handbook of Plato*, ed. G. Fine, 88–113. New York.

McDonald, R. 2001. *Shakespeare and the Arts of Language.* Oxford.

McPherran, M. L. 1990. "Kahn on the Pre-Middle Dialogues." In *Oxford Studies in Ancient Philosophy*, ed. J. Annas, 211–236. Oxford.

———, ed. 2010. *Plato's* Republic: *A Critical Guide*. Cambridge.

Mheallaigh, K. N. 2008. "Pseudo-Documentarianism and the Limits of Ancient Fiction." *American Journal of Philology* 129:403–431.

Michelini, A. N., ed. 2003. *Plato As Author: The Rhetoric of Philosophy*. Leiden.

Morgan, J. R. 1993. "Make-Believe and Make Believe: The Fictionality of the Greek Novels." In Gill and Wiseman 1993:175–229.

Morgan, K. A. 2000. *Myth and Philosophy from the Presocratics to Plato*. Cambridge.

———. 2004. "Plato." In *Narrators, Narratees, and Narratives in Ancient Greek Literature*, ed. I. J. F. de Jong, R. Nunlist, and A. Bowle, 357–376. Leiden.

Mulhern, J. J. 1971. "Two Interpretive Fallacies." *Systematics* 9:168–172.

Nagy, G. 1990. *Pindar's Homer*. Baltimore.

———. 2004. *Homer's Text and Language*. Urbana.

Nails, D. 1995. *Agora, Academy, and the Conduct of Philosophy*. Dordrecht.

———. 2002. *The People of Plato: A Prosopography of Plato and other Socratics*. Indianapolis.

Nehamas, A. 1985. *Nietzsche: Life as Literature*. Cambridge, MA.

Nettleship, R. L. 1901. *Lectures on the* Republic *of Plato*. 2nd ed. London.

Nietzsche, F. 2010. "On Truth and Lie in a Nonmoral Sense (1873)." In *On Truth and Untruth: Selected Writings*, trans. T. Carman, 15–49. New York.

Nightingale, A. W. 1995. *Genres in Dialogue: Plato and the Construct of Philosophy*. Cambridge.

———. 2002. "Distant Views: 'Realistic' and 'Fantastic' Mimesis in Plato." In Annas and Rowe 2002:227–247.

———. 2004. *Spectacles of Truth in Classical Greek Philosophy: Theoria in Its Cultural Context*. Cambridge.

Norris, C. 1983. *The Deconstructive Turn: Essays in the Rhetoric of Philosophy*. London.

Palmer, F. R. 1986. *Mood and Modality*. Cambridge.

Pappas, N. 2013. *Plato and the* Republic. 3rd ed. New York.

Penner, T., and C. Rowe. 2005. *Plato's* Lysis. Cambridge.

Portner, P. 2009. *Modality*. Oxford.

Press, G. A. 1993a. *Plato's Dialogues: New Studies and Interpretations*. Lanham.

———. 1993b. "Principles of Dramatic and Non-Dramatic Plato Interpretation." In Press 1993a:107–127.

———. 1995. "Plato's Dialogues as Enactments." In Gonzales 1995:133–152.

———. 1997. "The Dialogical Mode in Modern Plato Studies." In Hart and Tejera 1997:1–28.

———. 1998. "The State of the Question in the Study of Plato." In Smith 1998, 1:309–332.

———, ed. 2000. *Who Speaks for Plato? Studies in Platonic Anonymity*. Lanham.

———, ed. 2012. *The Continuum Companion to Plato*. London.

Prince, G. 2003a. *A Dictionary of Narratology*. Revised ed. Lincoln.

———. 2003b. "Surveying Narratology." In Kindt and Müller 2003:1–16.

Quirk, R. et al. 1972. *A Grammar of Contemporary English*. New York.

Ramsey, F. P. 1990. *Philosophical Papers*. Ed. D. H. Mellor. Cambridge.

Reeve, C. D. C. 1988. *Philosopher-Kings: The Argument of Plato's* Republic. Princeton.

———. 2004. *Plato. Republic*. Indianapolis.

Rescher, N. 1991. "Thought Experimentation in Presocratic Philosophy." In *Thought Experiments in Science and Philosophy*, ed. T. Horowitz and G. Massey, 31–41. Lanham, MD.

Richards, I. A. 1965. *The Philosophy of Rhetoric*. Oxford. Orig. pub. 1936.

Ricoeur, P. 1981. *Hermeneutics and the Human Sciences: Essays on Language, Action, and Interpretation*. Ed. J. B. Thompson. Cambridge.

Riginos, A. S. 1976. *Platonica: The Anecdotes Concerning the Life and Writings of Plato*. Leiden.

Rimmon-Kenan, S. 1983. *Narrative Fiction*. London.

Rose, P. W. 1992. *Sons of the Gods, Children of the Earth: Ideology and Literary Form in Ancient Greece*. Ithaca.

Rowe, C. 2003. "Review: Plato and Socrates." *Phronesis* 48.3:248–270.

———. 2006. "The Literary and Philosophical Style of the *Republic*." In *The Blackwell Guide to Plato's* Republic, ed. G. Santas, 7–24. Malden.

———. 2007. *Plato and the Art of Philosophical Writing*. Cambridge.

Rutherford, R. B. 1995. *The Art of Plato: Ten Essays in Platonic Interpretation*. Cambridge, MA.

———. 2002. "Comments on Nightingale." In Annas and Rowe 2002:249–262.

Said, E. W. 1975. *Beginnings: Intention and Method*. New York.

Salkie, R. 1988. Review of *Mood and Modality* by F. R. Palmer. *Journal of Linguistics* 24.1:240–243.

Sayre, K. M. 1995. *Plato's Literary Garden: How to Read a Platonic Dialogue*. Notre Dame.

Schaeffer, J.-M. 2009. "Fictional vs. Factual Narration." In *Handbook of Narratology*, ed. P. Hühn and W. Schmid, 98–114. Berlin.

Schaerer, R. 1969. *La Question platonicienne: Étude sur les rapports de la pensée et de l'expression dans les dialogues*. 2nd. ed. Neuchatel.

Schleiermacher, F. 1836. *Introductions to the Dialogues of Plato*. Trans. W. Dobson. London.

Schmid, W. 2003. "Narrativity and Eventfulness." In Kindt and Müller 2003:17–33.

Scholes, R. 1985. *Textual Power: Literary Theory and the Teaching of English*. New Haven.

Schur, D. 1998. *The Way of Oblivion: Heraclitus and Kafka*. Cambridge, MA.

Scott, G. A., ed. 2007. *Philosophy in Dialogue: Plato's Many Devices*. Evanston.

Shorey, P. 1937. *Plato. Republic*. 2 vols. Rev. ed. Cambridge, MA.

Slings, S. R., ed. 2003. *Platonis Rempublicam*. Oxford.

Smith, N. D., ed. 1998. *Plato: Critical Assessments*. 4 vols. London.

———. 2007. "Plato's Book of Images." In Scott 2007:3–14.

Snell, B. 1955. *Die Entdeckung des Geistes*. 3rd ed. Hamburg.

Spitzer, L. 1988. *Interpretive Essays*. Ed. A. K. Forcione et al. Stanford.

Stanzel, F. K. 1984. *A Theory of Narrative*. Trans. C. Goedsche. Cambridge.

Stefanini, L. 1949. *Platone*. 2nd ed. Padua.

Stout, J. 1982. "What Is the Meaning of a Text?" *New Literary History* 14:1–12.

Strauss, L. 1964. *The City and Man*. Chicago.

Szlezák, T. A. 1985. *Platon und die Schriftlichkeit der Philosophie: Interpretationen zu den frühen und mittleren Dialogen*. Berlin.

———. 1997. "Schleiermachers 'Einleitung' zur Platon-Übersetzung von 1804." *Antike und Abendland* 43:46–62.

———. 1999. *Reading Plato*. Trans. G. Zanker. London.

Tennemann, W. G. 1792. *System der Philosophie*. Vol. 1. Leipzig.

Thesleff, H. 2012. "Pedimental Structure of the Dialogues." In Press 2012:121–123.

Tigerstedt, E. N. 1974. *The Decline and Fall of the Neoplatonic Interpretation of Plato: An Outline and Some Observations*. Helsinki.

———. 1977. *Interpreting Plato*. Stockholm.

Todorov, T. 1977. *The Poetics of Prose*. Trans. R. Howard. Ithaca.

———. 2007. "What is Literature For?" Trans. J. Lyons. *New Literary History* 38:13–32.

Trask, L. 2007. *Language and Linguistics: The Key Concepts*. 2nd ed. Ed. P. Stockwell. New York.

Vaihinger, H. 1924. *The Philosophy of "As If": A System of the Theoretical, Practical, and Religious Fictions of Mankind*. Trans. C. K. Ogden. London.

Vendler, H. 1988. *The Music of What Happens*. Cambridge, MA.

———. 1997a. *The Art of Shakespeare's Sonnets*. Cambridge, MA.

———. 1997b. "The Time-Chain of Emotions: Ideas into Forms in Sonnet 30." http://harvardmagazine.com/1997/09/poets.html.

Wakker, G. 1994. *Conditions and Conditionals: An Investigation of Ancient Greek*. Amsterdam.

White, N. P. 1979. *A Companion to Plato's* Republic. Indianapolis.

Wolfsdorf, D. 1999. "Plato and the Mouth-Piece Theory." *Ancient Philosophy* 19:13–24.

———. 2004. "Socrates' Avowals of Knowledge." *Phronesis* 49.2:75–142.

Index